W9-BFD-905

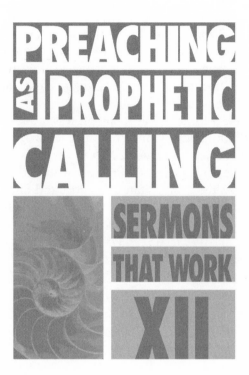

PREACHING AS PROPHETIC CALLING

SERMONS THAT WORK XII

EDITORS

Roger Alling is president of The Episcopal Preaching Foundation, and director of the Foundation's widely acclaimed Preaching Excellence Program for students in Episcopal seminaries. He has edited each of the twelve volumes in *Sermons that Work*, this anthology series committed to the celebration and nurture of preaching in the Episcopal tradition. He has been a parish priest and diocesan stewardship officer. Currently he serves as a priest associate in both Pennsylvania and Southwest Florida.

David J. Schlafer is a former philosophy professor and seminary sub-dean who has taught homiletics at four Episcopal seminaries and The College of Preachers. He has led seminars at Methodist, Presbyterian, Lutheran, and Baptist seminaries. He devotes primary energy to leading conferences on preaching across the United States, Canada, and England. He has written *Surviving the Sermon: A Guide to Preaching for Those Who Have to Listen; Your Way with God's Word: Discovering Your Distinctive Preaching Voice*; and *What Makes This Day Different: Preaching Grace on Special Occasions*. Soon to be published is *Playing with Fire: Preaching Work as Kindling Art*.

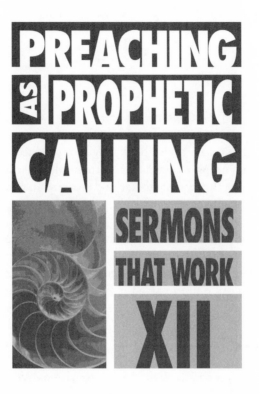

PREACHING AS PROPHETIC CALLING

SERMONS THAT WORK XII

Edited by
Roger Alling and David J. Schlafer

MOREHOUSE PUBLISHING
A Continuum imprint
HARRISBURG • LONDON • NEW YORK

Copyright © 2004 by Roger Alling and David J. Schlafer

Morehouse Publishing
P.O. Box 1321
Harrisburg, PA 17105

Morehouse Publishing is a Continuum imprint

All rights reserved. No part of this book may be reproduced or transmitted in any form or by any means, electronic or mechanical, including photocopying, recording, or by any information storage and retrieval system, without written permission from the publisher.

Unless otherwise noted, the Scripture quotations contained herein are from the New Revised Standard Version Bible, copyright © 1989 by the Division of Christian Education of the National Council of Churches of Christ in the U.S.A. Used by permission. All rights reserved.

The Scripture quotations from the Revised Standard Version of the Bible (RSV), copyrighted 1946, 1952, (c) 1971, 1973, are used by permission.

Scripture taken from the Holy Bible, New International Version, copyright © 1973, 1978, 1984 by International Bible Society is used by permission of Zondervan Publishing House.

Library of Congress Cataloging-in-Publication Data

Preaching as prophetic calling / edited by Roger Alling and David J. Schlafer.
    p.   cm. — (Sermons that work ; 12)
  ISBN 0-8192-1893-6 (pbk.)
  1. Episcopal Church—Sermons. 2. Sermons, American. I. Alling, Roger, 1933–
II. Schlafer, David J., 1944– III. Series.
  BX5937.A1P743 2004
  252'.0373—dc21

                                              2003013484

Printed in the United States of America

00 01 02 03 04 05   10 9 8 7 6 5 4 3 2 1

PREACHING AS PROPHETIC CALLING

2 Framing Spacious Visions of Prophetic Ministry

Describing Dimensions of Prophetic Speech

Uplifting Elements in Prophetic Leadership

Affirming the Corporate Nature of Prophetic Witness

Providing Fresh Reminders of Uncomfortable Truths

Offering Unsettling Insights into Familiar Texts

Reorienting the Faith Community Toward Resurrection Life

3 *Preaching Paul Prophetically*

Introduction: The Range of Riches in "Prophetic" Preaching

IN A RECENT e-mail exchange, a seasoned colleague expressed his perception of—and frustration with—the dearth of prophetic preaching he has encountered since the September 11 attacks, and the ensuing advent of "The War on Terrorism":

> Over the past few months I have become increasingly discouraged with the preaching I hear going from parish to parish. Regardless of denomination, it has become banal and palliative in the worst sense of that word. God is screaming through the events of our times, and no one is hearing. Fear and anxiety have gripped the Church and denial is the current state (unless it is fundamentalist, in which case the anxiety takes the form of self-righteous pugnacity).[1]

What a stark and sobering indictment on the enterprise and its practitioners! And yet, a stimulus, as well, for preachers to reconsider one of the significant challenges of their profession: to speak difficult truths in dangerous times. If all that preachers do is proclaim peace when there is no peace (or incite holy wars to combat holy wars), then they only join a long line of disreputable "court prophets," those who rubber-stamp, in religious language, the policies of a self-serving status quo. Whatever a preacher's prophetic task, it *isn't* simply telling people what they want to hear.

But what *does* "prophetic preaching" look like? Pictures of various "prophet" figures prominent in public consciousness come spontaneously to mind:

- Strange-looking, street-corner figures, folks with wild eyes, scruffy beards, tattered clothes, and bony fingers. Speakers with raucous voices, clamoring "Repent or Burn!"—telling people not what they want to hear, but where they're going to go. Speakers whom passers-by tend simply to shrug off with a giggle or a snort.
- More esoteric figures, exotic, even—horoscope writers, crystal-ball gazers, palm readers, séance conductors, those whose loyal followers find the paranormal fascinating.
- Figures who command even wider followings—meteorological forecasters, economic prognosticators, political pundits—those whose

---

1. Message from Ron Cebik, Deacon in the Diocese of Connecticut.

reputations ebb and flow with the constant changes of their respective batting averages.

- Another kind of figure comes to mind as well: the prophet as passionate advocate, speaking out on behalf of children, wetlands, endangered species, the economically or physically disadvantaged—the spokesperson for important but neglected causes. (And the partisan lobbyist who, employing similar language, sincerely or self-servingly, pushes special interest in the name of principle.)

Does the prophetic preacher look like any of these? A number of biblical prophets would certainly have been so perceived by those among whom they spoke. Samuel, Elijah, Ezekiel, Jeremiah, Hosea, Amos—each and all of these seem, in one context or another, to "fit the picture."

Yet the association of these "prophet" images with any of those prophetic individuals is superficial at best. The vocation of a prophet may, on occasion, take concrete form in shrill speech, odd manner, prediction of future events, or vigorous, partisan advocacy. Much more essential to being prophetic, however, is a gift and a burden—the ability to see and speak of ordinary events with extra-ordinary insight:

- To see things with everyday eyes—and then to look again, seeing them now as they *really are* (as Amos was coached into doing when he gazed upon a basket of summer fruit).
- To hear various voices, and come to understand, as Samuel did, which is the voice that matters most deeply, and where it is coming from.
- To have lips purged and touched for speaking, as did Isaiah and Jeremiah. And then, having drawn a deep breath, to speak clear words. Not words that tell folks what they want to hear, but words that enable listeners to see and to say for themselves something that is utterly essential to their health and healing.

"Thus saith the Lord!" No preacher (save an arrogant one) rises readily to make such a claim. But to preach at all is necessarily to imply it, although in fear and trembling. It is a responsibility no preacher can beg off from, citing humility or inadequacy. Speaking for God, however haltingly, comes with the territory.

But how one goes about doing so is not easy to understand, let alone to undertake. "The word of the Lord was rare in those days," says the biblical chronicler, setting the scene for the call of Samuel. The pessimistic e-mail assessment of the current state of preaching seems, in somewhat different language, to be claiming something similar. *If* this is so, *why* is it so?

Perhaps to some extent because preachers aren't listening to what God is screaming through the events of our time. Or maybe because preachers do not have the courage to say what they see and hear.

But part of the difficulty in speaking as a prophet surely lies elsewhere. There are elements in prophetic speech that render it *inherently* problematic. These elements can be named as a series of tensions, distinctive but related, that no one called to prophetic speech can ever escape. Consider:

- Complex issues demand more than the clear expression of strong convictions. Careful research and reflection are important aspects of prophetic address. Preachers need to do their homework with open minds. Thoughtful analysis and assessment take time. And surely it is important for the preacher, having studied an issue with care, to share those findings in the sermon itself.

  So far, so good. *And yet,* if the time allotted for sermon *delivery* is filled full with quotations, statistics, and case studies, it is quite possible that the proclamation of the Gospel itself may be overshadowed—buried in political, economic, and sociological detail. Sound theological reflection requires solid social analysis. But social analysis and critique do not equate to theological understanding.

- If preachers avoid taking positions on controversial topics, their sermons, sooner or later, begin to sound like unhelpful platitudes and vague spiritualizing generalizations (Peace is better than war! The environment must be protected, but so must jobs as well!)

  And yet, taking controversial stances in sermons is risky business, and not just because it may prove unpopular with one constituency or another. A congregation is, if not a captive, at least an essentially receptive audience. It doesn't get the chance, in the moment (at least in many churches) to answer back, to respond "Yes, but . . . ." There is always more to be said, and on another side, than can or should be presented in any sermon. The God of Scripture takes positions, exercises "preferential options." But seldom, if ever, does God simply pontificate, shutting down dialogue over matters of ultimate importance. Bully pulpiteering is not prophetic speech. There is, therefore, an ever-present tension between taking clear, firm stands and creating broad, hospitable listening spaces for alternative points of view.

- If sermons never issue *specific* calls for *particular* action, that silence is a thunderous testimony, not to the God of Incarnation, but to a God of infinite abstraction. A word that never calls for strategic, costly action is *not* a witness to The Word Made Flesh.

And yet, prophetic calls to action ("He has no hands but our hands . . .") often smack of moralistic Pelagianism, self-generated salvation, rather than Saving Grace. How can a preacher, in the same sermon, speak meaningfully about both taking initiative in the name of the Lord and (in humble recognition of human inadequacy) "waiting upon God"?

- If preachers stress (as well they should) the *corporate, communal* character of Christian responsibility, listeners can find wiggle room to underestimate their duty as *individuals.* (What, after all, can *I* really do about it?)

  And yet, placing heavy emphasis on personal responsibility can easily lead to the impression that individual effort is not just *necessary* but *sufficient.* A faithful preacher will choose prophetic words with care, of course. But different ears hear the same words in different ways. Getting it right is a daunting, if not impossible task, with respect to the relationship between responsibility that is "mine" and that which is "ours."

- If preachers do not consciously take the time to map out and focus upon social issues of significant moment, their preaching will present an insular, myopic view of God's Righteous Realm.

  And yet, the systematic setting of "prophetic" agendas can be perceived as, or actually fall into, axe grinding. Worse still, it can, with the best of intentions, impose interpretational agendas on biblical witness. Eisegesis is always questionable, regardless of how justifiable may be the cause in which it is enlisted.

- If preachers are not sensitive to issues of prophetic import, the Gospel will come to sound irrelevant to the raw, conflicted, tortured places where nations and peoples live.

  And yet, if "what the Gospel calls us to do" becomes an all-consuming preoccupation for the preacher, then the situation-transcending, life-transforming essence of God's good news of new life in Jesus Christ may become distorted or altogether lost. The Realm of God has decisive practical implications for human society; but no human social order is equivalent to the Kingdom of Heaven.

"In each case, strike the proper balance" is the obvious rejoinder to this daunting list of concerns. But that, of course, is easier said than done. How do preachers deal with such paradoxical tensions creatively?

The sermons in this volume are cases in point of how members of the company of preachers can attempt to shoulder the burden and celebrate the gift. They suggest that prophetic artistry may be learned more effectively by way of "taste and see" than by receipt of a recipe. Still, the variety of expression presented here does manifest a certain pattern and shape.

Broadly, the sermons you will be hearing as you read can be clustered around two related but distinctive tasks, the complementarities of which are doubtless apparent:

- *Focusing Specific Issues of Prophetic Concern*, and
- *Framing Spacious Visions of Prophetic Ministry*

The first dimension has to do with "where the rubber meets the road," with "the what, the where, and the when" of preaching prophetically. The second dimension has more to do with the lay of the land, with the overall "how and why" of prophetic preaching. What both dimensions have in common is the primary concern for naming rather than blaming, with describing more than prescribing. Every sermon in this volume, in other words, speaks, in one way or another, a word of judgment. Right judgment, however, is not judgmental. It is always a word of discernment, rather than a word of condemnation.

Alan Jones has well observed: "The first law of the spiritual life is attention." Whatever the prophet focus may say about what we should do, therefore, is always framed in the descriptive context of what *God* has done, is doing, and promises yet to do.

Hence, even in "Focusing Specific Issues of Prophetic Concern" (Part 1), we believe that *celebrating signs of hope* takes a certain theological precedence over *naming needs and challenges*—critical to our faithful participation in the Inbreaking Realm of God though these needs and challenges surely are. For it is only as we see how God *has* acted and *is* acting that we can both perceive where God is leading and find the appropriately empowering energy to follow.

Several aspects are involved in the basic dimension of "Framing Spacious Visions of Prophetic Ministry" (Part 2). The *dimensions of prophetic speech itself need to be described.*

Even more than being delineated, however, *prophetic leadership needs to be uplifted*, for information without inspiration seldom produces significant modification!

Change activity in service of the Realm of God is a communal undertaking. Hence the importance, particularly in a cultural setting charged with individualism, of *affirming the corporate nature of prophetic witness*.

Speaking hard (not harsh) words does not devolve, for the preacher, from a position of personal, professional, or vocational privilege. The whole of the faith community stands under the Word of God, a word often uncomfortable, and unsettling, and strangely unfamiliar, regardless of how well known. It is only as the church opens itself to *fresh reminders of uncomfortable truths,* and to *unsettling insights into familiar texts,* that it finds prophetic energy and direction for addressing needs and challenges.

All prophetic dynamic moves both from and toward the ultimate world remaking that we name as Easter. Thus, the continual *re-orientation of prophetic preaching must be toward Resurrection Life.*

Selected for their particular "taste" and vision, rather than because they conform to any pre-established pattern, these sermons nevertheless, both individually and taken together, say something of what we believe the rich range of "prophetic preaching" encompasses. Not only is there variety of topic, style, and approach here. There is alternative, even conflicting, interpretation as well. (Listen, for example, to two very different ways in which the Canaanite woman sounds through sermons deliberately juxtaposed, one upon the other!)

Sermons delivered at the Episcopal Preaching Foundation's annual Preaching Excellence Conference have, this year, been dispersed throughout the volume, rather than gathered into a separate section.

In the last volume of this series, Katherine Grieb began a careful investigation of how preachers can effectively undertake the task of preaching from the Letters of Paul.[2] Now she trains her sights more specifically on the prophetic dimension of Paul's own proclamation, and what contemporary preachers can learn from him as they shoulder that task—always a challenging undertaking, but particularly daunting at this time in the life of the nation and the world. There has always been, in this long-running anthology series, a deep resonance between the sermon conversations convened around the topic of the volume and the spirit of the essays included therein. In the present volume, the focus of Dr. Grieb's essay honors not just the general spirit, but also the explicit letter. Her essay is a distinguished contribution to the emerging literature on "Pauline Homiletics," one for which the editors are deeply grateful and exceptionally proud to present to sermon listeners, practicing preachers, and theological professionals alike. We are also pleased that, in her essay, Dr. Grieb addresses the work of a preacher who had already been selected for inclusion in this volume's conversation about prophetic preaching.

Once again, the editors have the duty and privilege of expressing thanks to Morehouse Publishing for its significant and gracious investment in giving sermons that work a wider hearing.

---

2. "Preaching from the Pauline Epistles: Problems and Possibilities," in *Preaching: Through Holy Days and Holidays: Sermons That Work, XI* (Harrisburg, Pennsylvania: 2003), 88–110.

1

CELEBRATING SIGNS OF HOPE

COMMUNITY SERVICES

A Table in the Wilderness

Psalm 78:14–20; Romans 8:35–39; Matthew 14:13–21
Proper 13 A
Amanda Rutherford May

THE LAND AROUND the Sea of Galilee is hardly a wilderness. It is rich and fertile country with beautiful hills and valleys and some trees. Yet Jesus speaks of withdrawing to "a lonely place." The words translated "lonely place" in Matthew's Gospel literally mean "a place that is like a wilderness." The wilderness—a place of quiet, of stillness, of barrenness— a place that is wild and open, a place where we come to terms with ourselves and with God.

The wilderness experience of the people of Israel was the most formative in the Old Testament. After having been led out of slavery in Egypt by Moses, the Israelites wandered in the wilderness for forty years. Forty years of moving toward the Promised Land, forty years of trusting in God, trusting in God to protect them and to guide them, trusting in God to satisfy their hunger and to assuage their thirst. In the wilderness they experienced hardship and freedom, and they longed for comfort and slavery. They were tempted to worship other gods and to turn back to the life from which they had been redeemed. But God loved his people. He taught them, fed them, and cared for them. Finally when they were ready, God led them to the Promised Land.

The story of the loaves and fishes is the story of another wilderness experience. After Jesus was rejected in his own city of Nazareth, the disciples brought him the news that John the Baptist had been executed. For all of them it was a time of failure and fear. They left Nazareth and crossed the Sea of Galilee to a "lonely place"—a wilderness where they could again come to terms with themselves and with God. But when they arrived, the people of Galilee, like the Israelites of old, had gathered to experience God, to escape from the slavery of sin, and to seek the Promised Land, the kingdom of God proclaimed by the Messiah. Jesus taught the people, as God had taught the Israelites in the wilderness. He cast out demons and healed the sick, as God had cared for the Israelites in their wanderings. But as the day lengthened and the people began to be hungry and restless, even the faithful wondered: "Can God prepare a table in the wilderness?"

On that day in Galilee, there were only five loaves and two fishes, a meal for *one* to feed a crowd of *five thousand* men, besides the women and children. Jesus took the offerings, blessed and broke them, and gave them to the disciples to feed the people. In the Exodus, God fed the people of Israel with manna and with quails, enough for the whole company each day. But on that day in Galilee, the people were fed and there was food left over—more than enough for all to share. Like the Israelites of the Exodus, the people of Galilee and the disciples who had sought out "a lonely place" experienced God in their midst, a loving and faithful God who prepared a table in the wilderness with food and drink in abundance.

I have had the privilege for the last eight years of serving as the executive director of Episcopal Community Services. This agency provides services to the poor in San Diego and Riverside Counties, including:

- early childhood education and care
- drug and alcohol rehabilitation, education, and prevention
- housing for battered women and their children, and for women who have themselves been offenders
- emergency assistance
- services and housing for the homeless mentally ill
- employment for the homeless and for foster youth entering the workforce
- housing for those who are homeless and suffering from AIDS
- chaplaincy to all of our programs

With five hundred employees and forty locations, our programs serve about thirty-five hundred clients each day.

ECS is a place where we experience wilderness. Those who come to us are physically, mentally, and spiritually in the wilderness of their lives. Some have nowhere to sleep; some have no food; some are mentally, physically, or spiritually ill. Many are addicted or abused. All are poor. Many have been separated from families and friends for years. Some are separated from God. Like the Israelites of old, they wander, looking for the Promised Land, trying to rely on God's providence, yet asking the question, "Can God prepare a table in the wilderness?"

Bob had enjoyed a successful career. As a young man he had graduated from Stanford, then completed an MBA at Harvard. He had become a marketing executive in a succession of companies, with a significant income, a house, and a bright future—bright, until the clouds started to form. He was unable to perform at his usual high standards and eventually didn't go to work at all. His company terminated him. He found himself unable to search for a new job. As money got tighter and tighter, his wife left him, defeated by his undiagnosed disease. Bob lived in his house for two years, spending all his savings, until the bank foreclosed, the utility companies cut off services, and his friends deserted him.

As he will tell you, one day he was carrying a bucket of water from his swimming pool to the bathroom to flush a toilet, because the water had been turned off. He said to himself, "Bob, this is crazy! And if this is crazy, you must be crazy too!" Shortly thereafter he was forced out of his house and was forced to live in his car. When his car was finally repossessed, Bob found himself homeless and living on the street. For Bob it was the wilderness, a time of powerlessness, desperation, fear, and loneliness. He could not overcome the situation, and he could not escape. It was all he could do to survive.

Eventually Bob found his way to the ECS Friend-to-Friend Clubhouse, where he could shower and eat and talk to others who were mentally ill. Bob suffered from a form of clinical depression so severe that at times he could not function. After he was diagnosed and the appropriate medications were prescribed, Bob began to return to a shadow of his former self. He started by working at the ECS Downtown Work Center for minimum wage. He then joined the ECS staff, working as a counselor at the Friend-to-Friend Clubhouse. From there he became the manager of the Work Center. But he was still too fragile, and he sank into depression again. It was a low point for all of us who had great hopes for Bob's recovery. But, he returned to his job at the Clubhouse and slowly has been restored to health. About three years ago, he accepted a new job at his old salary scale, doing marketing on the Internet.

On his last day at the Clubhouse, Bob gathered together the members to tell them his story and the good news. Now those who are members of the Friend-to-Friend Clubhouse are homeless (or nearly homeless) and mentally ill. They hear voices, they are depressed or manic, they are paranoid or delusional, but they come together at the Clubhouse to form a community. There is a great bond among the members of the Clubhouse. They know they are fragile. They know they are outcasts. They know that their futures are uncertain. But they also know that at the Clubhouse they are respected and treated with dignity, valued because they are children of God.

Bob told the members that he was going to a job that paid a hundred thousand dollars more than his job at the Clubhouse. They thought he was delusional. Then he told them that he was buying a new industrial strength washer and dryer for the Clubhouse. That was enough to convince everyone!

The going-away party was joyful, festive, and full of hope. In the midst of the wilderness of fear and loneliness, oppression and degradation, God had prepared a table for Bob and his friends at the Clubhouse. Bob told me as he was leaving that he would never forget what ECS had done for him: that we had helped him and believed in him, but most of all that we had convinced him that God had not forsaken him.

To be in the wilderness is to be apart. To experience the wilderness is to experience separation. It is a place stripped of amenities. It is a place forsaken. And when we enter into a wilderness experience, we take on the nature of the place. The comfort of our daily lives is removed. We feel suddenly very alone, very vulnerable, and very much in the presence of God.

All of us spend time in the wilderness. Perhaps we have been homeless, addicted, or abused. Perhaps we have been depressed, despairing, in mourning. Perhaps we have felt worthless, useless, or ineffectual. Perhaps we have felt abandoned or betrayed by friends, family, or by God. But that time we spend in the wilderness is a time to be cherished, for it is a time when we come face to face with God. It is a time when pretensions are stripped away and we come to know that indeed God will provide for us—and that we cannot provide for ourselves.

Several years ago I went to the Holy Land, and in the course of visiting different places in Israel, I went to the small monastery where the miracle of the loaves and fishes is commemorated. It is a wilderness, not without water or greenery, as it sits on the shore of the Sea of Galilee, but a place where there is silence and the presence of God. On the floor of the sanctuary is a second-century tile floor with the symbols of the loaves and fishes. Around the sanctuary are the Eucharistic words describing Jesus' action as he was given the meager offerings of bread and fish. "Jesus took the bread, blessed it, broke it, and gave it to the crowd," the words of the Last Supper and the words said every Sunday in our Eucharist together.

For each of us the Eucharistic words are reminders of that encounter with God in the wilderness, for it is there that we offer ourselves to God, and there that he takes up the offering of our lives. God blesses us, and calls us his children. He breaks apart our worlds to conform our wills to his. And he gives us to the world for service in the name of Christ.

It is hard to say what it was about that monastery that influenced my own spiritual journey, but it was from that time and place that I mark my adult commitment as a disciple of Christ. Perhaps it was that my intellectual resistance to Christianity was finally broken down by the historical reality of that simple place. But looking back over the years, I know that God called me from the wilderness of my life at that time to experience his presence, the presence of a loving and faithful God. For me, God prepared a table in the wilderness, and it was in those simple Eucharistic words written on the walls of the sanctuary that I found my life in God.

"Can God prepare a table in the wilderness?" The stories of the Old and New Testaments and our own experiences echo with a resounding "yes!" For each of us the time in the wilderness is a time of struggle, a time of waiting and watching, a time of vulnerability. But it is in the wilderness, where all is stripped away, that we know the power of God's love.

As Paul wrote in his letter to the Romans: "For I am convinced that neither death, nor life, nor angels, nor rulers, nor things present, nor things to come, nor powers, nor height, nor depth, nor anything else in all creation, will be able to separate us from the love of God in Christ Jesus our Lord." It is in the wilderness that the table is prepared for us, and it is there that God gives us the Bread of Life.

Amanda Rutherford May is executive director of Episcopal Community Services, San Diego, California.

LITERACY

Finding a Voice

Luke 18:1–8
Proper 24 C
Margaret A. Faeth

DURING A RECENT family vacation, I caught a cold that turned into laryngitis. For an entire week I had no voice. It became a long and lonely week as I was progressively isolated by my inability to speak. For the first day or two, my children still expected some response from me. I clapped as my son bravely attempted his first back dive. When my daughter asked for a Popsicle before dinner, I was able to get my message across with a shake of my head and a raised eyebrow. But I missed a lovely bike ride because nobody heard my response to the invitation. Before long we were all tired of the extra effort it took to communicate. Nobody wanted my germs, but I really missed my daily dose of hugs and kisses. I became more isolated as the children began to look to their father as the sole source of permission, affirmation, and response.

I became very dependent upon my husband. I couldn't introduce myself in the church we visited. I couldn't ask directions or use the telephone. I couldn't even make my own doctor's appointment. In restaurants, after much gesticulating and pointing, I finally had to have Paul order for me. I began to understand what it must feel like to be invisible. I really don't know what I would have done without my husband. In my voiceless state, he was my advocate, the one who bridged the chasm between society and me. In the midst of my frustration however, I realized that my condition was only temporary. I knew that soon I would be able to speak for myself.

Two thousand years ago, women did not have the luxury of speaking for themselves. In ancient Palestine, women relied exclusively on the men in their lives for permission, affirmation, and response. Virtuous women lived in isolation, venturing out into public only under swaths of veils designed to protect their modesty. A good woman was *not* seen and *not* heard. Jewish folklore explained that the mother of the Maccabean heroes had been blessed with so many valiant sons because even the beams in her ceiling had never seen a hair of her uncovered head.

In a society so unaccustomed to the sight and sounds of women, widows posed a special problem. A woman fortunate enough to have sons became dependent upon them after her husband died. Some women were taken in by male relatives. But the widow without a male advocate lived on the outskirts of society—without voice and without hope. The Greek and Hebrew words for widow reflect this isolation. The Hebrew word for widow, *almanah,* comes from the word that means mute or voiceless. The Greek word for widow, *chera,* is derived from the word *chasma,* which denotes a chasm or deficiency.

Voiceless, deficient, isolated by an impossible social chasm—this was the widow's reality. The big surprise in today's Gospel is *not* that the judge grew weary of the widow's persistence and relented. The big surprise is that the widow *found her voice.* She sought justice and mercy when she had no right or reason to expect it. Under Jewish law, she had no right to be heard. Had she been wealthy, or the mother of sons, she would have found an advocate to present her petition. But this was apparently not the case. In her desperation, she cried out across the chasm of social norms that isolated her. If we listen carefully, we can still hear the echoes.

My friend Ginny knows the pain of isolation. Without an advocate in the public school system, she advanced from grade to grade without learning to read. In the eyes of her teachers and classmates, Ginny's deficiency defined her. Labeled stupid and slow, she became an outcast. In humiliation, she finally dropped out when she turned sixteen. She began a series of menial jobs that she undertook with her usual sense of quiet determination. You might know Ginny. She's the one who scrapes the food off our plates when we finish our restaurant meal. She's the one who dries our hubcaps at the carwash. And when her illiteracy is discovered, Ginny is the voiceless, helpless one who falls victim to employers who alter or miscalculate her timecard, double charge her for uniforms, and reduce her wages because she can't tell the difference.

Ginny knows the cry of desperation. Her isolation drove her into a relationship with the first man who paid her any attention—an advocate at last. But it *didn't* last. Finally, alone and without an advocate, Ginny gave up her only child for adoption because she didn't understand the paperwork she was asked to sign.

It took a long time, but Ginny's pain and isolation finally pushed her to the edge of the chasm and she called out for help. Her past had taught her that she had no right or reason to expect a response, but her petition was answered. At age forty, Ginny found her voice when she learned to read. Literacy was the bridge that Ginny built, word by word, book by book, between herself and society. Ginny's efforts were sustained by her longing for God. Her dream was to worship in a Christian community without shame, able to follow the pastor's instructions to open her Bible to a particular chapter and verse. God listened to Ginny as nobody had listened to her before. In grace, God responded with a wealth of opportunities beyond Ginny's wildest dreams. Before the ears of mercy, Ginny learned to speak for herself.

The voiceless live around us and among us. Some stand wistfully, isolated by social conventions that they did not create, but do not know how to surmount—things like hunger, fear, injustice, and oppression. Why are they so often overlooked—unheard? Perhaps one reason is that their situations serve as stark symbols for a fact that is difficult to face—that, truth be told, each one of us lives on the edge of one kind of chasm or another.

Some stand defiantly, relying on their own power and will to bridge the gap. But if we dare to look into the ultimate chasm—the abyss of sin, we become dizzy with the realization that we can't cross that chasm alone.

Jesus' instructions to pray always and not to lose heart are reminders that, before the ears of a loving God, his people have found their voices. Throughout history, God has responded to the cries of those who had no right to be heard: the poor, the captive, the outcast, the sinner. When the chasm became impassable, God became one of us and crossed over to the other side so that the isolated and the needy could know the height, depth, and breadth of redeeming love. A love that extends a welcome to the voiceless and the desperate—to you and to me. A love that invites our participation through faithful prayer. Prayer joins our deepest longings with God's highest purposes. In prayer we find our voices—praising, pleading, and penitent. In prayer we give voice to the echoes that plead for justice and mercy, joining our own limitations with the power of God.

Jesus, our Advocate and Guide, leads us across the chasm from isolation into communion, from deficiency into wholeness, from death into life.

Margaret Ann Faeth is associate rector of Immanuel Church on the Hill, Alexandria, Virginia.

PRISON MINISTRY

Living Bibles

1 Corinthians 12:27–13:13; Luke 9:28–36
Last Sunday after the Epiphany, Year C
Lynn Christophersen Woodward

THE REMARKABLE experience of transfiguration told by Luke begins in the mundane. Peter, John, and James "knew" Jesus. They had walked all over the Middle Eastern countryside with him for almost three years. They knew what Jesus was like in the mornings when he first woke up, what he was like at the end of a long day. They had feasted together, commiserated together, disagreed and encouraged one another. They had established the routine of their life together and everyone pretty much knew his part. Yes, there had been some startling moments: miracles, talk of suffering. But then the dust had always settled. Day-to-day routines continued. Walk a little, teach a little, heal a little, pray a little. Humans naturally settle into routine, with inertia against disruption. Please do not disturb. Just let me be. Change? No, thank you. Not today.

To go off to a quiet place for prayer was part of the routine. Peter, John, and James knew what was going to happen. Perhaps they felt relief. It would be a time of restful dozing, away from the hum of humanity that always seemed to surround them. They knew what to expect.

I imagine Peter looking up lazily from his dozing, at what he expected to see: Jesus in prayer. Suddenly Peter's eyes open wide as he sits up. There is Jesus, his face lit with an inner radiance, his clothing dazzling, and two other figures as well. Peter nudges John and James. "Look! Moses and Elijah!" The disciples shade their eyes from the brilliance. Peter exclaims, "I understand! Jesus is not merely our rabbi! He is as great as Moses and Elijah! Let's memorialize this event by building a monument."

God responds immediately: "This is my Son, marked by my love. *Listen to him!*"

Peter, John, and James never saw Jesus quite the same after that. I believe *they* never looked quite the same to the other disciples after that—or that the other disciples looked the same to *them*. Things were changing.

"Listen to him!" God's words echo in the disciples' ears. "Listen to him." God is telling us not to build external monuments, but to listen to Jesus. Learn from Jesus how to grow God's love in our hearts. Learn how to be living testaments—to be marked by God's love. "Listen to him!" God invites us into the Son's Transfiguration.

My own experience of transfiguration has been fairly gradual. A few people experience more instantaneous transformations. I think of Peter, and Paul, Mary of Nazareth, and Mary of Magdala. More recently, I think of my friend Jami. Jami's transfiguration was immediate and profound. She continues to be a part of my more gradual transfiguration.

Jami was a guest on Oklahoma's first Kairos Outside weekend, a weekend for women who have family members and/or loved ones in prison. The routine includes a series of talks by women sharing their life journeys. The guests respond to the talks in small groups at tables. The team spends many hours building Christian community before each weekend. The Kairos Outside slogan is "Listen! Listen! Love! Love!" The team seeks God's help in building a loving environment where the guests can experience their own transfiguration.

Few of us on that first weekend in Oklahoma had experienced a loved one in prison. Some of us had volunteered inside a prison. Only the leaders had observed an actual weekend. I was serving as a table leader. We were seated seven to a table: an assistant table leader, five guests, and I. My work was to facilitate discussion after each talk.

I first met Jami in letters that came with her application to attend the weekend. She wrote several, all of which said pretty much the same thing. She'd walked the line with her "ol' man" for more than twenty-five years, most of them at "the walls." That meant she'd been visiting her husband, Jesse, in the maximum-security prison for most of her life. They were very young when he was convicted. She couldn't imagine what some Christian women who hadn't done the hard time like she had could possibly say to her. Jami was coming only, *only,* because Jesse insisted. You see Jesse had been on a Kairos weekend inside the prison. And there was something different about him.

The weekend began on a Friday evening after work. I knew Jami had arrived at the retreat center by the buzz among the team members. We each had been assigned a guest to welcome. She wouldn't allow her team member to carry her overnight bag to the room.

I didn't actually see Jami until we gathered in the dining room. She is almost as tall as I am. Her face is what I noticed first. I couldn't see her eyes because she wore wrap-around sunglasses that she kept on all evening. The blush on each of her cheeks was a slash mark of color. War paint came to mind. She wouldn't sit at the table with us. She always sat with her back against the wall—alone. And she watched. Even with the shades on, the impression of her watchfulness was overwhelming. Never had I experienced the intense scrutiny we all felt from Jami that first night. Jami watched and she listened.

We all prayed that God would show us how to be with this woman. At one point, a team member went and simply sat near her. They exchanged a few words. And Jami watched.

That night after our guests went to bed, we had our team meeting. Now was the time to assign guests to the small groups at the tables. I remember praying, "Oh, please God, don't let Jami be assigned to my table." I wondered what on earth I could possibly say to her. I was so new to this journey of having a family member in prison. That hardness I saw frightened me. I listened to the names of the guests at my table being announced. Ruth, Rita, Melissa, Laura—Jami. I took a deep breath, gulped and said: "Okay, God. What was that you said? Oh, right. Listen, listen. Love, love."

I've since learned that during that first night, about three A.M., Jami was sitting outside her room. She was thinking about leaving. One of the team members came and sat with her. Jami asked about this prayer thing. "How do you do it?" The woman gave her a paper with the name "Jesus" printed on it and told her simply to trace his name with her finger and speak each letter out loud. Jami stayed.

In the morning after breakfast, we gathered in the community room. The table leaders sat down at their tables. The guests' names were called out and they sat down. Jami sat across from me, her back toward the wall, still unsmiling, still wearing the sunglasses. We listened to several talks. In our discussions afterward we shared pieces of our own stories, considered what we had heard. Jami listened very intently. She asked a few questions—different questions. At one point she pushed her shades up on her head, looked at me, and asked, "You walk the line to visit your ol' man. How come you're not hard? How do you stay soft?" Once more, like Peter, I said something inane. I believe one of the guests jumped in and responded to her question.

"God, what is my part in this?" I prayed.

Little by little, though, those tendrils of God's love were working their miracle in Jami. After the talk on "isolation and rejection," we all knew something was happening. The speaker gave her talk, we discussed, then took a break. Jami and the speaker communicated by notes.

When we sat down for the next talk. Jami began to tremble, then cry. "What's happening to me?" she whispered. The other table leader put her hand on Jami's back. Her crying reached a deeper level. We helped her out of the room to a sofa in the hall. Jami collapsed at our knees and we held her. The speaker and a spiritual advisor came out. Jami was told about Jesus, and about God's transforming love. All I could think was, "Here is a beloved child of God who is terrified." I stroked her forehead and face as words of comfort and love were spoken to her. She wept and wept— tears that had been held back for years.

She began to smile through her tears. "You all have lights in your eyes!" she exclaimed. "What is that?" "That's Jesus' love for you," we told her. We all laughed for joy with this newly found child of God.

At one point, her face clouded and she began to weep again. "Will they let me go back in? I've made a commotion." The speaker said, "Jami, do you know what people are doing in there this very moment? They are praying for you!" We were all awash in tears again.

Jami looked different when she re-entered the room. Yes, her eyes were red-rimmed, but the shades were on top of her head, and by dinnertime they were left in her room. Her smile lit up her whole face and she glowed! At dinnertime, she sat with us at a table with her back to the middle of the room. If joy is the infallible sign of the presence of God, Jami was filled to overflowing.

That was two years ago. Jami knew she needed to find a Christian community, a church home. I'd like to tell you that happened easily, but it didn't. Too many churches thought they "knew" Jami and turned her away. She finally found a community that looked at her through transfigured eyes and welcomed her. The other day we were talking on the phone. "Lynn, you're not gonna believe this!" she said. I laughed. "Jami, you've taught me that with God all things are possible." She will be giving the message at Penn Avenue/Redemption Methodist Church in Oklahoma City next month.

I will be working on the next Kairos Outside team with Jami. At our first team meeting, we were asked to introduce ourselves by telling about a favorite Kairos Outside highlight. Jami said, "When I first came to Kairos, I didn't even know what the Bible was. You all were my first Bible." And then she went around to each one of us and told us what Bible lesson we had taught her. She concluded by saying, "My first Bible was you all—living people."

Jami is a living testament to the transfigured Christ. I have watched her be the good news to everyone she meets. We are invited to become living Bibles. We let God mark us with God's love. We become the Gospel—the only Bible some people know. Are we willing to let our walk with Jesus change us, transform us? What is written on our faces if someone looks to us? Will they see good news?

Lynn Christopherson Woodward is deacon
at St. Michael's Church, Norman, Oklahoma.

HOSPICE CARE

Dreamers

Luke 6:20–26
The Feast of All Saints
Scott P. Albergate

TODAY WE observe the Feast of All Saints, that grand occasion on which we remember heroes of the Christian faith in days past. Today, I would like to remember a "local saint" who spent her life not very far north of here in Hawthorne, New York. If you take a drive through Hawthorne, you come upon the place where she lived and worked. It surprises you when you first see it, rising out of the lush landscape lining the highway. The place is a lovely group of Spanish-style buildings on several acres. It is the sign on the highway that slows you down, or stops you altogether: *"Rosary Hill Home: Operated by the Servants of Relief for Incurable Cancer."*

"What kind of a place is this?" you ask. More than a few people, myself included, have found themselves backing up their vehicles and entering the grounds to satisfy their curiosity. When you knock on the door of the Rosary Hill Home, you are greeted by a Roman Catholic nun. Inside you find more like her, two dozen or so. And you come to learn that these nuns spend their lives at Rosary Hill Home caring for cancer patients who can't afford nursing care, who are uncared for by our system of "managed care," and who have come to the final stop on the health care line.

Inquiring further, you learn that these caretakers of the "suffering poor" are women caught up in a dream, the dream of another woman who lived long ago. That woman is Rose Hawthorne, born in 1851, daughter of the famous writer Nathaniel Hawthorne, and founder of the Rosary Hill Home. In the days of Rose Hawthorne, in nineteenth-century America, people believed that cancer was contagious. If you contracted cancer, you were banished from your family, shunned by your friends, and left to die without medical or spiritual care in a "poor house." You died in misery, and you died alone.

In 1891, Rose Hawthorne was forty years old, living alone and in her own kind of misery. She had just separated from her alcoholic husband, ending an unhappy marriage of some twenty years. Rose became aware of the plight of incurable cancer patients and was inspired to do something about it. She moved from Boston to New York in order to train as a practical nurse. She converted to Christianity. But she was restless and felt possessed by a dream: to do something more for the victims of cancer. She dreamed of giving these outcasts from society a home where they could be cared for. In a bold move to find funding for her dream, Rose Hawthorne wrote a book about her famous family. To her surprise it became a bestseller. With the royalties, Rose acquired a tenement in the lower East Side of New York City and opened it to cancer patients.

Ten years later, after the death of her husband, Rose became a Roman Catholic nun and founded the religious community known as the Servants of Relief for Incurable Cancer. She also opened Rosary Hill Home here in Westchester County to expand her pioneering work with cancer patients. And this was in 1900, long before there was a hospice movement, long before anyone cared about caring for the dying.

Rose never charged any money for the care she gave the patients; and to this day, the Servants of Relief for Incurable Cancer will not accept payment of any kind, nor will they accept federal funding, Welfare, Medicaid or Medicare, or gifts from patients or their families. The nuns at Rosary Hill Home will explain to you that "suffering cannot be managed;" but that what *can* be done is to spread the "Gospel of Love" of Jesus Christ. For them, there is no price for giving the gift of compassion.

Rose Hawthorne died in 1926. Her legacy is the seven homes like Rosary Hill that operate today in six states. No miracles are performed at these homes. No one who goes as a patient ever leaves. All these nuns do is give a final earthly home to these suffering poor people. That's the legacy of this local saint.

Rose Hawthorne is not an official canonized saint of any church. But she is a saint, nonetheless, at least according to the best definition I've ever heard. It comes from Alan Jones, the dean of Grace Episcopal Cathedral in San Francisco: "Saints," Father Jones says, "are those persons whose lives are so transparent to God that God's light shines through them into the life of the world, and into its structures, organizations, and programs."[1]

---

1. Alan Jones and Rachel Hosmer, *Living in the Spirit*, The Church's Teaching Series (Minneapolis, Minnesota: The Seabury Press, 1979), 217.

People like Rose Hawthorne inspire us because their lives are so transparent. Through their bold dreams we can catch a glimpse of the dream God has for the world. God does have a dream for a better world; and we are meant to be caught up in that dream.

Few of us ever think about becoming saints. Maybe it's because we think that saints were mythical figures, who lived incredible lives and did seemingly impossible things. But a modern saint like Rose Hawthorne reminds us that the only barrier between us and sainthood—between an unfulfilled life and a life transparent to God—has to do with how we *think* about life.

Saints think "outside the box." They think not of limitation, but of possibility. Saints believe in the art of the possible. They seize life against the odds. Think about it: just what were the odds that a penniless, nineteenth-century woman, separated from her husband, would create a revolution in the care of cancer patients as Rose Hawthorne did?

On this day we remember all the heroic, saintly people who have gone before us. People like our own St. Luke who wrote a Gospel about Jesus. People like Rose Hawthorne. People like the ones who founded our church and have sustained its life through the past century.

Funny thing about saints, though. We always tend to remember them for what they *did,* for their accomplishments. Perhaps it would be more useful for us to recall that saints were not just *doers.* They were *dreamers* first. Saints: dreamers first, doers second. Today reminds us that we are called to become part of that "community of dreamers," living transparent lives so that the light of God can shine upon the world.

Scott P. Albergate is rector of St. John's Church,
Compass, in Gap, Pennsylvania.

RECYCLING

Broken, Blessed, Redeemed

Luke 22:14–30
Maundy Thursday
Susan Palwick

"THEN HE TOOK a loaf of bread, and when he had given thanks, he broke it and gave it to them, saying, 'This is my body, which is given for you. Do this in remembrance of me.' " These words, the Institution of the

Lord's Supper, are the source of the Eucharistic prayer we hear every Sunday. The Eucharist carefully follows that same four-fold pattern: the priest *takes* the bread, *blesses* it, *breaks* it, and *gives* it to the congregation.

Take, bless, break, give. The more you think about that pattern, the stranger it becomes. Why would you bless something, only to break it? Why would you give as a gift something that was broken? Most of us don't want broken presents. If something's broken, we throw it away. It becomes garbage. *[Lift trash bag, containing an object the congregation can't see yet.]* And the more beautiful the gift was in the first place, the more distressed we are if it's been broken by the time it reaches us.

Many years ago, a dear friend of mine, who lived thousands of miles away, sent me a beautiful glass vase as a birthday gift. I opened the box, saw the exquisite hand-blown glass, and was delighted—only to realize, when I lifted my new treasure out of its packaging, that it had broken in transit. My friend had carefully chosen the gift for me; she'd blessed it and sent it into the world, where it broke. I mourned the fact that the vase wasn't whole any more, and I regretfully threw it away. But how would I have felt if my friend had chosen the lovely object, blessed it, smashed it, and put it into a gift-wrapped box?

Well, I probably would have thought she was crazy, or else that she hated me. Sane people—at least outside the church—don't bless things and then break them. People who love you don't give you garbage as a gift. That simply isn't done. It's not the way of the world.

I remember the way of the world very forcefully whenever I go hiking on Peavine. If any of you have been up there, you know that, along with lovely scenery and wildlife and lots of fresh air, the mountain is home to garbage. *[Heft trash bag.]* A lot of garbage: old cars and trucks, refrigerators, washing machines, television sets. People haul that stuff up onto the mountain and dump it; then they use it for target practice. Most of those former major appliances have so many holes in them that you can hardly tell what they used to be.

I'd gotten used to the cars and washing machines. And then one day my husband found this. *[Lift ruined head of bass fiddle out of the trash bag]* This is the head of a bass fiddle. Its body, kicked and caved in and shot to pieces, was lying several yards away from this smaller piece, which my husband brought home. We looked at it and scratched our heads. Maybe somebody got really frustrated with music lessons? Maybe somebody's auditions didn't go well? There's a story here, that's for sure, but we'll never know what it is.

What we do know, what we can tell just by looking at this ruined object, is that whoever broke it didn't bless it first. The pattern here isn't *take, bless, break, give*. The pattern here is *take, curse, break, throw away*. That's the way of the world, especially here in America, with its malls and its consumer culture. The way of the world is so familiar that we hardly see it anymore, hardly comment on it. It can take something as startling as an assassinated bass fiddle on Peavine—or as shattering as the ruins left behind by a suicide bomber—to make us wonder if there isn't some other way, some better way.

Whoever built this instrument loved it. It was designed to be beautiful and to create beauty; it was designed to be part of a whole, part of a band or an orchestra. And then it fell into the clutches of someone who hated it, who cursed it and broke it and discarded it. Look at the splintered wood. Look at the holes gouged into the neck. That much damage didn't happen by accident. It was deliberate. It was planned. And it took a lot of force. *[Drop bass fiddle back into trash bag—**thunk**. Put bag on floor.]*

We're here on the eve of the darkest day in the Christian calendar, the day when the most beautiful thing in the world will be broken, nailed to a piece of wood, and discarded on a hillside. That horror was already planned, already inevitable, when Jesus said that first Eucharistic prayer; and he knew it. He was trying to tell his disciples, too, but I wonder how much they allowed themselves to hear. "This is my body, given for you." Did any of them except Judas grasp how literal that phrase was about to become? Did they truly realize that the crisis was only hours away, or did they think that Jesus was just using metaphors again, speaking in parables?

Much later, after the wonder and terror of the Resurrection, the disciples *will* understand what he was saying. Later, they'll realize that he was already trying to comfort them. "My body will be broken, but it will be a gift, too, the best gift you've ever gotten, the gift that brings new life. Just wait and see."

They can't possibly understand that yet, on Maundy Thursday. And they won't be able to understand it on Good Friday, when all they'll know, all they'll be able to see or smell or taste, is their grief.

We understand it now, don't we? We listen to the words every Sunday: *take, bless, break, give.* Of course we know what they mean: we've had almost two thousand years to think about them. Well, I'm not so sure. If we really knew what they meant, I think there might be less garbage on Peavine. If we really knew what they meant, I think there'd be more people like Kate McDermott and Jon Rowley, who got married last summer, and who asked for such an unusual wedding gift that it got written up in *The New Yorker.*

Kate and Jon are gardeners. To celebrate their marriage, they asked their friends to send them garbage. People sent them coffee grounds, banana peels, dryer lint, pulp from juice bars, and a box of buffalo poop, among other things. Kate and Jon, who have both been married before, used these unlikely gifts as compost to help nourish a wedding rose bush. "We are recycled ourselves," Kate says. "We're taking all the life experience that most people discard and turning it into something bountiful and full of new life."[1]

Clearly, these are Easter people: they know about resurrection, about broken things producing new life. They know that redemption is, both simply and profoundly, God's way of recycling, of saying that nothing has to be garbage, that nothing needs to go to waste, that not a sparrow falls but is counted. But how do you make sense of all that when it's not even Good Friday yet? What do you do when you're heading into the darkest time you've ever known, or are already in the middle of it? What do you do when you feel broken yourself?

I've come to believe that the Eucharistic prayer is not just a pattern, but a promise. I think it's God's way of reminding us that when we feel broken, we can be gifts. I think it's God's assurance that if we feel broken, we've already been blessed, instead of cursed. We can only feel broken when we have first been whole; we grieve most deeply the loss of what has given us the greatest joy. The hard part, our work as Christians, is to remember the prior blessing and to reach for the future gift. Our work as Christians is to find loving alternatives to the cursing, discarding, despairing way of the world. Our work as Christians is to be co-redeemers with God.

This sanctuary contains a poignant reminder of that work. On Christmas Eve, 1934, a young woman was killed in Berkeley, California, when her bicycle brakes failed on a steep hill. Her father, Frederick Graves, was the vicar of St. Stephen's. He must have felt broken beyond all reckoning; what parent wouldn't? But if his grief included cursing and despair, we have no record of it. What we have instead is the altar he carved as a memorial, on which he inscribed the words, "Erected to the glory of God in gratitude for the joyous life of Mary Graves Dunn." In his pain and brokenness, Frederick Graves remembered the blessing of his daughter's life, and he turned his family's grief into a gift. Our Eucharistic table is itself a kind of Eucharist.

"Do this in remembrance of me." When you listen to the Eucharistic prayer this evening, think about the gifts that you, too, have created out

---

1. "Bridal Registry: Will You Mulch Me?" "Talk of the Town" section of *The New Yorker*, August 13, 2001, 26.

of grief and darkness. Only you know what they are. But whatever they are, they are a true remembrance of Christ the Redeemer, whose will it is that nothing go to waste.

Susan Palwick is a lay preacher in training at St. Stephen's Church, Reno, Nevada, and Associate Professor of English at the University of Nevada, Reno.

NAMING NEEDS AND CHALLENGES

CHRONIC POVERTY

Beetles

John 9:18–41
Lent 4 A
James B. Cook

IN HIS BOOK, *The Power of the Powerless,* Christopher de Vinck tells this simple story:

> One spring afternoon, my five-year-old son, David, and I were planting raspberry bushes along the side of the garage . . . A neighbor joined us for a few moments . . . David pointed to the ground . . . "Look Daddy! What's that?" I stopped talking with my neighbor and looked down.
> "A beetle," I said.
> David was impressed and pleased with the discovery of this fancy colorful creature. My neighbor lifted his foot and stepped on the insect giving his shoe an extra twist in the dirt. "That ought to do it," he laughed.
> David looked up at me, waiting for an explanation, a reason . . . That night, just before I turned off the light in his bedroom, David whispered to me, "I liked that beetle, Daddy."
> "I did, too," I whispered back."[1]

De Vinck concludes the story by saying that "we have the power to choose."

---

1. Chrisopher de Vinck, *The Power of the Powerless* (Garden City, NY: Doubleday and Co., 1998), 3–5.

You and I have the power to choose how we will respond to every dancing, dying, exquisite, annoying creature that God sets before us.

Our responses, our choices matter. And sometimes, our feet move quicker than our hearts.

Consider the disciples, for example. They choose to step over the blind beggar and engage Jesus in a debate. "Rabbi," they ask, "who sinned, this man or his parents, that he was born blind?" They see a sinner, who is less important than their debate about the cause of his blindness.

Or, look at the Pharisees. They choose to use the blind beggar as a tool to trap Jesus for healing on the Sabbath. The man does not cooperate, however. "Whether he is a sinner, I do not know," he says out of frustration. "One thing I know, that though I was blind, now I see." Wrong answer! The religious elite cast him off. They excommunicate him.

The man's parents also make a choice. They decide to accept no responsibility for their son's new gift of sight, fearing separation from the synagogue if they show any loyalty to this Jesus by affirming their son's gift of sight. "He is of age; he will speak for himself," they respond.

All of them miss the point. Jesus is not interested in debating theology or the law. He chooses to approach and touch and heal a *man*, not a beggar, not a condemned sinner, not a pawn in an argument with the day's enlightened minds. And when the community shuns him, Jesus again seeks the man out and draws him even closer.

The choice to act with compassion does not elude Jesus as it does the disciples and the Pharisees, or as it can easily elude you and me. We need only to look at the suffering in this world to see that there are too many homeless, hungry, grieving, abandoned, frightened people—too many squashed beetles.

I am not sure why this is so, why human hearts are so full of blind spots, why our feet are so quick.

What I do know is that we cannot manufacture compassion. How often have we set out to love the world, or even more difficult, to love a classmate, a colleague, or a neighbor who is obstinate, belligerent, or irresponsible, and ended up feeling resentful, used, angry, and foolish ourselves?

Compassion is not a choice. It is a place in our hearts that holds the light and love of Christ.

The choice we make is to let Christ open our blind eyes and to join him on a life-long, heart-transforming journey. A journey filled with colorful, fancy creatures crossing our paths.

One such creature who crossed my path was introduced to me by my then three-year-old son, Nathan.

Nathan, Karen, and I are walking from my downtown office tower to the new Saks Fifth Avenue in Minneapolis to do some Christmas shopping. Nathan is wrapped in a snowsuit with a huge Paddington Bear smiling at us from the back of his coat. He chortles as the buses, the taxis, and the legs rush by.

"Look! A puppy dog!" Nathan shouts as he runs full steam ahead toward two shadowy figures perched in the florescent light of the Woolworth's display windows.

"Don't touch," I yell. "He's dirty."

Nathan has other plans.

"Nathan, stay away from there!"

He runs up to the dog and embraces him. The dog returns the signs of affection with his own: a swish of his tail, and a lick on Nathan's face.

The dog's companion is sitting on cardboard, his legs sticking out into the sidewalk, as he leans against the cold, stone building. His toes stick out from the black tennis shoes; his swollen, reddened ankles follow close behind. His blue, fur-lined parka is not zipped, exposing a fat belly from beneath a worn *Twins* sweatshirt. Dark, dirty, stringy hair frames his pocked and oily face. The hand on the dog's back has a small tattoo of a skull and bones. His fingernails are lined in black. He holds a bottle in a paper bag.

"Nathan, get over here. We have to get going," I say, looking at the dog to avoid the man.

"He must be freezing," I murmur to Karen. "It would help if he didn't drink."

"Oh, he's so cute," Nathan responds, infatuated with his new-found friends.

"He ain't gonna bite ya! Give 'im a pat!"

As Nathan pets the big mutt, I say a curt "Thanks!" to the man, and twist my shoe on the sidewalk as I turn away.

"Bye! See you later!" shouts Nathan, after one more hug for the dog.

Of course we did not see the man and his dog later. But they burn in my memory as a light that opens my blind eyes, and makes my heart to see.

I long to whisper in Nathan's ear, "I'm sorry about that beetle."

James B. Cook is rector of St. David's Church,
Minnetonka, Minnesota.

CAPITAL PUNISHMENT, GUN CONTROL

Independence Day

Ephesians 2:14
R. Lansing Hicks

DURING THIS Fourth of July week, I find myself singing again in my mind the words of an old hymn, a favorite during my Sunday school days. I haven't heard it recently for reasons we all understand. The first stanza goes:

Lead on, O King Eternal, the day of march has come;
henceforth in fields of conquest thy tents shall be our home.
Through days of preparation thy grace has made us strong;
and now, O King Eternal, we lift our battle song.

Remember it? Sure you do! But it's the second stanza particularly that keeps coming back to me when we celebrate the Fourth of July:

Lead on, O King Eternal, till sin's fierce war shall cease,
and holiness shall whisper the sweet Amen of peace.
For not with swords' loud clashing, nor roll of stirring drums;
but deeds of love and mercy the heavenly kingdom comes.

Throughout this holiday period, flags have flown and drums have rolled. Done in the right spirit, our celebrations are appropriate. It's natural that throughout this past week our thoughts turn to our country, which was "conceived in liberty"—achieving its independence through the blood, sweat, toil, and tears that accompany birth. The Fourth of July is indeed accompanied by "the roll of stirring drums."

But it's the other phrase from the old hymn that haunts me, for it is much more ominous: "swords' loud clashing." At this special time when we hear much about patriotism and national honor, we also hear the dreadful sounds of "swords' loud clashing" in Israel, Northern Ireland, Macedonia, Afghanistan. In one sense or another, the noise of battle is always ringing in our ears and swords are clashing loudly.

The older I get, the more convinced I become that war, not peace, is the natural human state. Among the earliest records of civilization, Egyptian and Babylonian, are victorious accounts of military conquests. Egyptian pharaohs, for instance, boasted century after century saying, "I smote the enemy with my sword." Jesus warned us that we would hear *wars and rumors of war.* I suspect that in the past fifteen hundred years of our Christian era there have been few generations without active conflict. Peace does not just happen when we have killed enough of our enemies to make the others surrender. That is only the cessation of hostilities. Peace takes work—the hard work of reconciliation.

So our hymn reminds us that it is *"not* with swords' loud clashing, nor roll of stirring drums; but deeds of love and mercy the heavenly kingdom comes." In the confusion of political and military propaganda today, it is not easy to think straight. When the flags are flying and the drums are rolling, it's hard to think soberly and clearly about true peace. But it is our duty, not only as Americans but also as Christians.

There is never a time when it is inappropriate to gather together for the purpose of peace. But as we come together for Holy Communion it is "meet, right, and our bounden duty" not only to pray for peace but to pursue it. Not just to worry about the absence of peace, but to work at creating conditions for peace. And this means standing up and protesting laws and legislation, men and movements, whose effects erode the bases of true peace and denigrate the humanity of any creature for whom Christ died. Therefore, let us be more specific. Let's come closer and talk about what's needed to create peace—for in a fallen world, it has to be created.

Two ingredients are necessary: the absence of conflict and the presence of reconciliation. In theory, the first, by itself, would seem better than its opposite, and better than nothing at all. Certainly the cessation of hostility is preferable to continued warfare. A quiet neighborhood appears more desirable than riots in the streets. But in practice it is not so. We know what happens in vacuums. A quiet neighborhood may mean an apathetic community, or one soon to erupt. The absence of military conflict—as now in Bosnia and Pakistan—does not create peace. Absence of hostility is not enough. Reconciling love must also be at work. It is not enough just to have forgiveness that is mere acceptance. We hear a lot from psychologists and psychiatrists about acceptance: self-acceptance and acceptance of others. But more than acceptance is needed. Commitment is needed as well. What is necessary is the type of reconciliation that works for unity, and building unity is hard work. It takes action, not just talk. In fact, it takes the kind of action that leads to death, death of self—sometimes even physical death. To establish real peace in any realm (military, sociological, personal), reconciliation is necessary.

Throughout the Bible, and highlighted in our text today, we see what that type of reconciliation looks like, the kind of love it requires, and the price it must pay: "For He is our peace . . . making in himself of the two one new person, so making peace . . . and reconciling both unto God in one body by the cross." Peace is costly.

The Epistle to the Ephesians, that marvelous document of peace and unity, makes two things clear: First, whatever the nature of our hopes and acts, Christ is our peace. He is both Model and Guide. For us who call him Lord, it is ultimately true that wherever we work for peace, we work in the spirit of Christ; and wherever we find peace, we find it by him and in him.

Second, however diverse our individual concerns for peace may be, the peace of Christ makes new persons. True peace brings unity, wholeness, and newness: As Paul declared, "If anyone be in Christ, they are a new creation."

Reconciling love involves not just attitude but action. It isn't enough to believe in good will toward all, or even to do good and to avoid evil. The Christian fight to which our hymn calls us is doing the right and protesting the wrong. Putting love into action means to act on both fronts: standing with those who are trying to reconcile the world by bringing healing and unity, and standing against all people and all things that cause fragmentation, hostility, and sickness.

The Church as an institution can show reconciling love through its policies and politics, by what it stands for and what it stands against at the corporate and official level, by passing resolutions, voted at our General Conventions. But each one of us can also take a stand as individuals. May I mention two of my own concerns?

My first concern is *capital punishment*. We have just recently shared with the world the shameful spectacle of our execution of Timothy McVeigh. The spectacle was covered by fourteen hundred reporters and round-the-clock TV programs: "All execution all the time."

Concerning his execution, some say justice was done, others that justice was not done. Both are wrong, for, in a case of murder, by what standard can we possibly measure justice? A life for a life? But McVeigh killed one hundred sixty-eight people. How then? Should we dig him up and inject him one hundred sixty-seven more times? Absurd! Or should we also execute one hundred sixty-seven of his family and friends? Preposterous! Should we just be satisfied to kill only him? But then we're back to the primitive standard of *an eye for an eye and a hand for a hand* that even the Old Testament rejected early on.

In a case of murder, or even multiple murder, what then? What are our alternatives? The mother of a four-year-old who was killed in the Oklahoma City bombing said on the day of McVeigh's execution that for her, justice had been done because she didn't want him able to kill others. So say we all! But life imprisonment without parole would accomplish that and not leave us with blood on our hands.

The day after McVeigh was executed, a man who had participated in the bombing of the American Embassy in Kenya was sentenced by a New York court to life imprisonment. He had killed two hundred thirteen people—many of them Americans. One person kills one hundred sixty-eight and is put to death; another kills two hundred thirteen and is given a life term! Which serves justice better? Such questions involve us in an infinite series of calculations for which we do not have adequate standards. But this may help: no European nation has capital punishment; banning it is a condition for membership in the European Union. Is their Christian conscience less refined than ours? By holding to the death penalty, the United States is increasingly separating itself from the democratic countries of the world.

The Christian view demands that justice be expressed through compassion, repentance, reconciliation, and restoration, as our text this morning states it. Will we stand up and say that, when and where it counts? On this Independence Day weekend, we are obligated to think about matters of life and death, about issues of conscience and morality.

On the day after McVeigh's execution, President Bush addressed the leaders of the European Union. He was immediately asked about America's position on capital punishment, and he answered that America is a democracy, and capital punishment is the wish of the majority of the American people. But we ask, on what grounds did he tell the leaders of Europe that the majority of Americans want the death penalty? Have we voted on this as a nation? The polls and resolutions I'm familiar with indicate the opposite. The Episcopal Church has voted strongly at our last three General Conventions to ban capital punishment.

My second concern is *gun control*. Last year over thirty-two thousand Americans were killed by guns. That's almost as much in one year as the total killed in Vietnam in seven years! By contrast, last year only one hundred twelve people were killed by guns in all of Europe, and Scandinavia. Do those people know something that we don't? Is their standard of morality higher than ours? Don't they get as angry as we do? Sure they do! Do they control their anger better than we? I doubt it! But they do control guns better than we do!

The NRA tells us, "Guns don't kill people; people do!" That's only half true, and a half-truth is the worst form of a lie. The full truth is "People kill people with guns!" If we are appalled that more than eighty Americans die each day—day after day—from guns, the least we can do is close the loophole that allows people to buy guns at gun shows without a background check. Throughout the two years following the Columbine massacre, during which sixty thousand Americans have died from gun violence, Congress has still refused to enact even such a basic reform as closing the gun show loophole. The citizens of the high-profile gun states of Colorado and Oregon took it upon themselves to close this loophole by direct vote after their legislatures refused to enact this common-sense reform. Little people can make a difference! If we support handgun control, we should stand up and say so!

I began by quoting the beloved old hymn, *Lead On, O King Eternal*. It warns us against the popular paths that lead to false peace, bought with the lives of others. In contrast, the Epistle to the Ephesians shows that the proper means to true peace is redemptive love that often involves death, as Christ reconciled us *through the cross*.

Today each of us will pray for peace in different ways. Tomorrow each will go out and work for peace in different areas—in family and community, in state and nation, for economic, social, and legal justice, justice in the workplace and justice in the courts. Remember the bumper sticker: IF YOU WANT PEACE, WORK FOR JUSTICE!

As we reflect on Independence week, when flags fly, drums roll, and swords still clash, may God grant us wisdom to understand true peace and clarity to see what it costs, and then give us courage to make peace, as he did, through redeeming love.

R. Lansing Hicks is professor of Old Testament, emeritus, at Yale Divinity School, New Haven, Connecticut.

CHILD VIOLENCE

Short Beds, Scant Covers, Narrow Doors

Isaiah 28:14–22; Luke 13:22–30
Proper 16 C
Roger Alling

THIS MORNING I want to talk about two theological questions and to discuss one pressing and tragic problem in our society. The theological questions are about prophecy and salvation. The tragic social problem is about children committing unspeakable crimes. These concerns are related.

Were the prophets of the Bible important because people thought they could see into the distant future? This certainly wasn't their first contribution. I believe their lasting importance lay elsewhere. What made the prophets important was their ability to see things in the present as they really were. It was their insight and their understanding that made the prophets special.

In the passage from the prophet that we read today, Isaiah complains that the nation has made a covenant with Death. Originally this referred to Hezekiah's attempted political alliance with Egypt, undertaken to try to overthrow the Assyrians. Isaiah clearly believes this to be a bad alliance, and calls on the king and the people to stand back from it. The culture of Egypt in that day was obsessed with death—hence the particular form of Isaiah's criticism.

When Isaiah looked out on his nation, he saw a people that had lost its way, and a culture that had become faithless and corrupt. He believed there would be a day of reckoning with God if the people did not repent and amend their lives. Isaiah then provides us with a wonderful image of a society, of a culture that has lost its way. He says: "For the bed is too short to stretch oneself on it, and the covering too narrow to wrap oneself in it."

Think about that for a moment. Have you ever tried to sleep on a bed that is too short? Have you ever tried to rest on a cold night with not enough covers to keep you warm? If so, you have a sense of what Isaiah is driving at.

Isaiah looked deeply into his own society and spoke of what he saw. With God's help, we need to look out at our own society so that we can see clearly and describe what we see faithfully.

In many ways our society and culture aren't working right, either. There is something terribly wrong in a society where children kill each other. The two incidents I have in mind specifically are the murders in Jonesboro, Arkansas, and the murder of the young girl in Chicago by boys, ages seven and eight. Unfortunately, these are not the only incidents of such violence. They are simply the ones most prominent in recent memory.

Events such as these trouble us all. They strike at the very heart of our society. They give us a sense of unease. They are like a bed that is too short and like coverings too meager to keep out the cold. Something needs to be done.

Before moving here, my wife and I lived in a suburb of Hartford, Connecticut. Several years ago we noticed that there seemed to be one or more youth homicides reported in the newspaper almost every day. Most of these were drug- or gang-related. Over time I came to realize that these events were challenging profoundly a value that had been an important part of my own upbringing. This value was the assumption that one did all one could to guard and protect children—one's own, of course, but the children of others as well. Now a new need was emerging. One had to think not only of protecting children and keeping them from harm's way, but also about protecting oneself—not just *for* the children, but in some cases *from* them. Outrageous! Surely these facts add up to a bed far too short and covers way too slim!

We will return to the social problem of children and crime. First, however, I want to say a word about the other theological issue in today's lessons—the issue of salvation.

As Jesus makes his way toward Jerusalem in Luke's Gospel today, a man stops him and asks a question about salvation: "Lord, will only a few be saved?" The answer Jesus gives is anything but simple. He uses the symbol of a door—getting through the door is a symbol for being saved. So far, so good. But Jesus continues, saying not one thing about the door, but three different things. He says that the door is narrow and that we should strive to enter through it. Then he says that under some circumstances the door is shut and can't be entered at all. Last, he says that the door is open and that people are entering it from north and south and east and west.

The person who put this question to Jesus probably thought he would get a simple answer, but he did not. The answer was complex. I think I can paraphrase the three things Jesus says in this way:

1. Salvation is important, so you don't want to miss out on it.
2. Salvation will challenge you, both in your thinking and your living, so don't think it will be an easy journey.
3. Salvation is intended for everyone, so don't be coming up with ideas that keep others out.

Furthermore, salvation is always more than one thing. You and I often think about salvation only as going to heaven where God's will is always done. We forget Jesus' teaching found in the Lord's prayer: "Your will be done on *earth* as in heaven." This phrase tells us much about the importance of salvation here and now.

What would salvation mean to children who are at risk today? What would it mean, both to those children who commit crimes and to those who suffer and die from them?

In answer, we can use Jesus' image of the door in the threefold way that he uses it in today's Gospel. First, the door is open. When children come into this world their lives spread out before them. Everyone hopes and prays that they will have life, liberty, and the pursuit of happiness. Everyone hopes and prays that they will come to love God and their neighbors as themselves.

But the *open* door is also *narrow*. We all make choices in life, even the very young. Choices have consequences, and some of the consequences that come upon us as a result of our choices can be very expensive. All of us need to walk carefully in the journey of life. There are significant risks and dangers on the way.

Sometimes the door is *closed*. The door for the earthly part of salvation is closed for the teacher and her students in Jonesboro, Arkansas. The door is closed for the little eleven-year-old girl in Chicago. In a different way the door has been closed for the four boys who were responsible for these two crimes. In countless ways, their lives will always be lived under the cloud of those horrible days. In this life some doors are shut in tragic and terrible circumstances.

Whatever is to be done about these terrible tragedies? People all over the country have been shocked by the murders in Jonesboro and Chicago. Our responses have been many and various. Some people simply throw up their hands in despair. They say, "It's a terrible situation but there is really nothing we can do about it."

Others adopt what I call the revenge-retribution response. Some states are suggesting more severe punishments for youthful offenders. Some have even proposed that children ten years old and older be incarcerated in adult prison facilities. We can only hope that saner notions will prevail. A recent study in Massachusetts demonstrated that stricter sentences and more punitive responses to youthful offenders have had no positive effect whatsoever on the problem of juvenile crime.

My own belief is that the only response that holds out hope is the one that attempts to change the culture in which we live. This is a huge assignment, but that may be proportionate to the dimensions of the problem.

What is culture? It is the totality of our social environment. Our culture holds us in the same way as water holds fish. We all live in it and none of us can escape. Now, our cultural water is polluted, which is a modern way of saying that the bed is too short and the bedcovers too narrow. When you have polluted water, it is imperative to clean it up.

In the *New York Times* a few years ago, Professor Moshe Halvertal made the following observation about crimes committed by very young people. "When we say that children are not fully legally responsible, one thing we mean by that is that they mirror the social life around them . . . They are naïve or in some ways transparent reflections of something in society—a certain violence, a certain cruelty. Without filtering, they represent what the society is about."[1] This is a terrible indictment of us if true. What is to be done? I believe that we need to attempt to effect change at every level of our society. We start with the individual. We can no longer assume that children born into our society are going to know and believe the most basic moral principles unless someone takes the time to instruct

---

1. *New York Times*, August 16, 1998.

them. I mean really simple things like respecting the lives of others even as you would respect your own life.

We then move on to the family, the church, the school, and the local community. These are larger units of family, and individuals need to be taught that the respect for others and their welfare is a part of what it means to be a human being. To change these things by helping individuals to see themselves and their welfare in these pictures is to change the culture. It is to change the way we think about ourselves and the way we think about the world in which we live.

Despair is not enough. Revenge is not enough. Individual moral development is not enough. We need to change the culture. The very bed needs to be made longer and the covers wide enough to cover us all. A culture of unrestrained violence makes everyone else a potential enemy. The atheist Jean Paul Sartre once said, "Hell is other people." If the culture of violence is never challenged, we will all live in implicit fear of each other.

A while ago a New York newspaper reported a story about a city neighborhood where crime had become a daily problem. Everyone lived in constant fear. When residents came home from work, they locked themselves in their apartments for fear of their neighbors. One day several people decided to cultivate a vacant lot with flowers and vegetables. As time went on, more and more of the neighbors joined in the effort. They began to know each other and they socialized a lot. One day they planted a tree in their new garden. They were very proud of all they had done. Then, one afternoon, a thief came and ripped up the tree and ran down the street with it. People came running from their houses, chased the thief, caught him, turned him over to the authorities and replanted the tree. The tree did not survive. What did survive, however, was a brand new sense of neighborhood and a commitment to a new way of human living.

That is working to change the culture. That is taking out the poison of the cultural water that holds us as the water holds fish. To do that is to make the bed long enough to sleep in and the covers wide enough to keep us all warm. It is to open the closed door and widen the narrow way that leads to salvation and to life.

Roger Alling is co-editor of this volume.

CHILD ABUSE

A Call to Remember

Genesis 9:8–17
Lent 1 B
Susan Salot Gaumer

THE DAY had been long and rainy, and the two-year-old was getting on her nerves! Food spilled, drawers emptied, the kitchen garbage strewn and walked through, a picture glass smashed as the child grabbed the forbidden object in defiance, screeching his only word: "No!"

"No! No! No!" was all she heard—besides the whining and crying. Crying without end. Pointless crying. Wailing, because he knew she hated it and could not abide it for long.

Without warning, rage engulfed her; and she was tearing into the garbage-strewn kitchen, headed for the miserable child. She caught him by his foot and jerked him into mid-air, turning him upside down, ready to . . .

A picture filled her mind, a picture of herself as a young child being flung against a wall by her own angered mother. She felt again the terror and the pain.

No! No! No!

She stopped, remembering the love out of which this child had been conceived, remembering the joy of his birth. She lowered him to the floor slowly, encircling her arms around his terrified little body, adding her tears to his. They hugged hard. She vowed never to treat him as her mother had treated her. Never, never, never—even though it meant accepting him for the little devil he had become.

It was a vow she would never break. Never. And in that vow, everything changed; a new universe was born. In that moment of remembrance, the world became a safe place where the child would grow up not as a scarred victim but as a cherished person at home in a grace-filled world.

They would begin again, this mother and her son. And the boy would learn that he could always depend on his mother because she loved him.

"I have set my bow in the clouds, and it shall be a sign of the covenant between me and the earth." With these words God laid down the weapon and embraced creation in a new and serious way, promising to be faithful to a renewed yet imperfect world, promising to love and abide a humankind that was still capable of destroying the goodness that God had created.

How God's heart had grieved, as Adam blamed Eve, and Cain slew Abel, and the life of Lamech brought only the promise of revenge and violence unlimited. "Only evil continually" was God's assessment of humankind before the Flood. And it broke God's heart.

How often have we encountered a child's picture book of Noah's ark—with happy animals, and Noah & Company, in raingear riding out the storm. Such versions have their place, but they distort our vision of this very adult story. For this tale is not primarily about boats or rainbows, or even about the remnant of Noah's faith, upon which God created anew. If a title were to be given to the story it might be called "The Broken and Changed Heart of God"—a heart described as devastated by human sin.

The Flood story is the story of God's change of heart, a change of relationship with humankind. From hostility to commitment. From retribution to acceptance.

God is revealed as the author of an ordered and predictable universe who will be faithful and who will never again—never, never again—break faith with all of creation, *with us.*

In the one, holy moment that God remembers Noah, the waters of forgetting subside and the earth is recreated, receiving anew the gift of God's limitless grace.

Out of the waters of forgetting we emerge, created anew. Washed free of any illusion that we belong to anyone other than God. Marked as Christ's Own Forever, inhabitants of God's heart.

"Do this in remembrance of me." With those words of God's beloved Son, God's renewing power is made present in our forgiven hearts.

"Do this in remembrance of me": a call to be signs of God's love in a world made imperfect by the human capacity for destruction of God's goodness. A call to cherish the children, and to hug hard the victims. A call to remember.

Susan Salot Gaumer is rector of St. Andrews Church,
New Orleans, Louisiana.

CLERGY SEXUAL ABUSE

Guarding the Sheep

Psalm 23; John 10:1–10
Easter 4 A
Lisa Sauber Mitchell

IT IS SAID that one day as Groucho Marx was getting off an elevator, he met a priest who immediately recognized the famous comedian. The excited clergyman extended his hand, saying, "I want to thank you for all the joy you've put into this world." Groucho shot back, "And I want to thank you, Father, for all the joy you've taken out of it."

Sadly today, those words take on a truth we do not want to hear—especially those of us who stand in pulpits and at altars across our land this day. We do not want to hear or acknowledge the possibility that we have taken joy out of life, acted inappropriately in our office, not rightly pastored those whom God has given to us. Should not the role of priest be precisely one of bringing joy into the world, in sharing the good news of God's wondrous, overflowing love? How could it be otherwise? Yet, sadly, it is so. Today the Scriptures call the Church and her leaders on their responsibilities; and if we will not listen to the voice of God, The Good Shepherd, then the Lord will find other ways to penetrate our eardrums and break into our hearts.

Today is Good Shepherd Sunday. You may have already picked up on this fact by the sheep metaphors in the lessons. I consider this day a kind of "comfort food" for the Church. The image of the Good Shepherd brings back memories of a safe and secure childhood. The Twenty-third Psalm, the *primo* comfort food of Scripture, places us back in the arms of gentle, protective, all-surrounding love.

Even in inconsolable moments of death and bereavement, fear and terror, when nothing else can soothe the soul, somehow the Twenty-third Psalm is a balm that begins the healing. The last time I spoke from this psalm was on the Sunday after Columbine, when we so needed words of safety and comfort. "The Lord is my Shepherd, I shall not want. . . ." How quickly these words bring us back to the center of who God is and to God's certain care for each of us.

We need to hear those words this morning. We need to hear of the shepherd who will lay down his life for the sheep, who will throw his body in the path of wild animals for our sake. We need to hear of the shepherd who comes to give us life and give it abundantly.

We all know the headlines in the news. The search for Osama bin Laden continues. The fighting in Afghanistan still rages. The Palestinian-Israeli conflict and its implications worry and frighten us. But something else has arisen that in certain respects far outshadows these horrors. It has invaded our safe havens, rocked our faith, reached into the fold of the Christian community, and revealed truths about ourselves we do not wish to see, know, or hear about.

Christians assume that the abuse of power, position, and authority will not happen within the confines of the faith community. How could it, if we are ruled by the rule of love? If our aim is selfless giving, with Jesus *himself* as our standard, how could we abuse one another? But it happens—even within the walls of the places we hold most dear. Although transgressing the appropriate boundaries of the shepherd's care by priests or church leaders is perhaps the most egregious and damaging violation of trust, we should be neither surprised nor naïve when it happens.

Jesus knew there would be thieves and robbers ready and waiting to climb into the sheepfold, dressed as shepherds, even speaking the language of shepherds. He also knew that they would not be true shepherds. Those who seek and follow Jesus need to learn how to be as gentle as doves, but also wise as serpents. Jesus knew that the Church he loves and died for would need to be vigilant in protecting the flock from those who enter to steal, kill, and destroy.

You have heard the stories of abuse that are circulating about our brothers and sisters in the Roman Church. The reactions have been many and loud. All Christians, regardless of church affiliation, know this is hideous. We all feel the pain of those who have been abused, then ignored, then dismissed.

Many quietly breathe sighs of relief: "Well, at least it's not *us*." But this is not just a "Roman" problem; it is a *human* problem. Any church that has human beings as leaders can find it. It *has* happened within the Episcopal Church and within this Diocese.

There are also those who may not see this as a "Roman" problem, but as a gay problem or a result of the rule of celibacy. I cannot say this too strongly: pedophilia has *nothing* to do with homosexuality or required celibacy. It is a sickness having more to do with the power of one person over another than with sexuality. Studies have found that most abusers of children are married men. This sickness is primarily an imposition of one person's will over another—an abuse of power—which is why crimes such as pedophilia and rape have, for generations, been part of war and conquest. Practiced among normally heterosexual men, this is abuse and forced submission, pure and simple. It is about the desire to exert one's own ego and to annihilate the personhood of the other. Please do not confuse the issues. There is enough confusion in our church and society without wrongly blaming those who are innocent.

Finally, there are those who are *glad* that the Church is in such trouble. Yes, glad! I'm not talking about those who are not Christians, or those who already had issues with Christianity before this story broke. I refer to those who think, "Now that the Roman Church is in such trouble, maybe people will leave it and find us!"

We are all part of the Body of Christ. When one member is injured, we are all injured. When one member grieves, we grieve *with* them. All of Christianity feels the burden of pain. All denominations share the weighty load that trusting believers, the young and most vulnerable, have been wounded. We have not done all we could do to protect the flock. Neither has the church done what is needful to give the perpetrators real help. They too are God's children, in need of God's redemption. They deserve better than to be allowed to continue in their sin. They deserve to be stopped—for their victim's sakes, certainly, but also for their own.

Should we excuse horrid, unspeakable behavior? Not at all. Jesus minced no words when he called them bandits and thieves. But let's not be naïve enough to think it could not be us. We may not commit the same sins that these priests are accused of, but *all* who are in positions of power and authority must examine themselves—and be examined by others. They must pray and renew fellowship with God daily, because where there is power and authority, there is always the possibility of abuse.

Such abuses occur in the secular world, whether in the monopolies of the nineteenth century or in the sweatshops and migrant fields of this century. Don't we cringe at the name Enron? Abuse of power. We have witnessed it over and over in our political system. And it can happen in the Church.

"Truly, truly I say to you, the one who does not enter the sheepfold by the door but climbs in by another way is a thief and a bandit; but the one who enters by the door is the shepherd of the sheep. The thief comes only to steal and kill and destroy; I came that they may have life, and have it abundantly." These words, "thief" and "bandit" are spoken to us, too. It is not just *somewhere out there.* Jesus tells us to be careful—yes, to have faith, to enjoy this fellowship and to cherish the Church—but also to be smart, to know that the healthiest of churches are not immune to abuses of power. Church leaders can stumble, lose focus, and seek their own interests rather than the interests of others.

I speak not only of bishops, priests, and deacons, but of all who serve in places of authority and leadership. All adults who sit in these pews are called to be good shepherds. For you really do the work of shepherd, in the way you lead and guide your own children, in the way you lead other children, consciously and unconsciously, by word and example. Like any priest, you represent the Church. By what you do and say, you speak for the Church and tell others, by who you are and what you do, what Christ is like.

I have no doubt that one of the main goals Jesus had was to equip his disciples, so that when he left them, they would be able to continue his work, spread the news of the Gospel, and survive in a world that was hostile to the message. Jesus was a realist; he wore no rose-tinted glasses. He knew the disciples would mess things up, make bad choices, that they would sin. Here he is, trying to give them what they will need to protect their flocks and to evaluate themselves. What kind of shepherds would they be?

This is the question all of us who are Church must ask today. Clergy and church leaders must look inward; but the call is given to *everyone* who has claimed the Christian faith, to look at why we are here and what we are doing. We must call each other to task, take our responsibilities seriously, and own up to those times when by our own actions, be they by accident or design, we have not been good shepherds, times when we have not laid down our lives, when we have looked after our own interests over the needs of others. Can it be said of *us* that we have taken joy out of life rather than brought it?

As I pray for my brothers and sisters in the Roman Catholic community, I cannot help but be cognizant of the fact that there have been many times when *I* have acted selfishly. There have been times when I have made faulty decisions, said things I shouldn't have said, times when I have *not* done and said things I *should* have. I tremble at the thought that many are the times when I do not stand with the Good Shepherd. I pray for God's forgiveness and pray that my actions have not caused insufferable pain in the lives of others. Can I stand and point my finger at the priests who abused their young charges? Can I bash the institution that then protected them at the expense of innocent souls? We must be very careful as we discuss these serious matters.

We can vow to do what we can to stop sexual abuse, to see that it does not happen again, that it does not happen here. We all must examine ourselves, take responsibility for the ministry in this place, and pray that the Good Shepherd will lead and guide.

This is Good Shepherd Sunday. No matter what happens in churches that are frail, flawed, human, let us never lose sight of the fact that we do, indeed, have a Good Shepherd. Jesus is his name, and he is Lord of lords, King of kings, Shepherd of *all* shepherds.

Terrible headlines? What do we tell our children? Must we talk about these unpleasant things? I believe it is a good thing that all of this has come out. It is the first step toward wholeness. It will allow reconciliation to begin. Will this tarnish the image of the Church? Certainly. But this is God's Church, we are his flock, and I cannot help but think that it is God who has broken this story. Yes, God, so that you and I, who might otherwise never talk about such things, are required to do so. We must talk about these things because we must take the position of Shepherd seriously and make sure that thieves and bandits do not break in and steal precious sheep.

At the end of my life I will be satisfied if I am acknowledged as one who brought joy into the world, if the Church I serve is known as a place of joy, acceptance, love, and safety.

May we tend the flock of God with joy and gladness and with the honor and respect that accompany this great privilege. May we tend the flock of God with earnestness and with the readiness to lay down our lives for these little ones—for the Lord is our Shepherd, we are his people and the sheep of the pasture, and he comes that we might have life and have it abundantly.

Lisa Sauber Mitchell is rector of Christ Church,
Shrewsbury, New Jersey.

AIDS

Speaking the Word

Mark 2:2–12
Epiphany 7 B
Sylvia Vasquez

I LONG TO speak the word, the word that has the power to lift us out of despair to hope, the word that can silence our fears and awaken us to rebirth. Shall I speak it? Utter it out loud? Dare I name it?

What is the one word you want to hear about AIDS? Is it the word *healed*? *Cure*? How about settling for *vaccine*? All are good words in the world of AIDS, words that give breathing space, a chance to save lives.

But is any one of these *the* word we need? Perhaps. Who could argue with the benefits of finding a cure or at least a vaccine? But good and helpful as these words are, what they represent is a long way off. In the world of those of us who have lived with AIDS, I think we need more—a word for more than medical relief, one that has a chance to undo all the damage that has been done to our human spirit.

Humanity has suffered with AIDS. I won't bore you with the statistics. Suffice it to say that the whole world suffers from this dread pandemic in one way or another. And as horrid as the physical pain and suffering are, the worst of AIDS does not happen to our bodies, it happens to our spirit.

What is this word we seek? For me, there is only one. *Love.* That alone can heal our wounds. Love is the only balm that will penetrate to the depths of our spiritual injury.

Those four men who brought their paralyzed friend to Jesus had to be motivated by love. Because only love can give us the stamina to hang around a friend or loved one who is desperately ill. Most people can do a good deed out of a sense of loyalty or good will. A lot of people are willing to take on the occasional volunteer job of caring for someone less fortunate. But only love outlasts duty, loyalty, or even justice. All those other motivators take us only so far. If we don't have love, however, we won't last as a care-giver or even as a justice-seeker for those who suffer from AIDS. Love alone will motivate us to continue to lobby for AIDS issues.

I want to tell you about a group of young men and women who were like the four who made a hole in the roof to bring healing to their friend. My brother Eddie had a great community of friends in Austin, Texas, many of whom were gay and lesbian. In the 1980s some of them became aware of the AIDS pandemic firsthand, because many were infected. As they learned more about AIDS, they realized that no information was being given to the Latino community in Austin, so they founded *Informe SIDA,* an AIDS information and referral agency. Through the work of that organization, they formed a close bond and determined to be there for one another as each faced death because of the virus.

I was in seminary at the time and met many of Eddie's friends. The Church had shunned most of them. They, in turn, claimed to be atheists. But you had to chuckle at their atheism. Eddie had a sign on his desk: "I am an atheist and I thank God for it!"

They didn't shy away from me, even though I represented an institution that had hurt them deeply. So we didn't talk about faith, or the Church, but I saw them *live* like Christian disciples. They shared material and emotional resources. They cooked for each other, bought medicines when the insurance companies denied claims, advocated for each other when EMS workers refused to take them to the hospitals. They cleaned for one another. They even wrote thank-you notes to family members who sent food or money, but did not feel free enough to share themselves.

Disease—that's another word to explore. If you say it slowly, it accurately portrays what happens to people when they come into contact with AIDS: *dis*-ease. The world has been uneasy with this disease. So uneasy that funding for research was very late in coming. A couple of months before he died, my brother asked me to watch a movie with him one evening, a movie he had taped so that he could leave our family some kind of documentation, some explanation for what had happened to him. Called *And the Band Played On,* the movie chronicled the early events leading up to the current AIDS situation. I was astounded at how much information was gathered and how quickly we could have addressed the AIDS crisis, had we moved earlier to educate and warn people.

So what was the source of the world's dis-ease with this disease? Why the hesitation? The world was uneasy because the early victims of this pandemic were gay men. Gay men: feared, misunderstood, hunted, tortured, gay men. The reason we didn't try to inform and warn the nation more quickly was that most people with the authority to act—didn't. And they didn't because the primary victims at the time were gay men.

Many of us gathered today have a lot of history with AIDS, either firsthand or indirectly. I am not an expert, and I often shy away from AIDS events because they are too painful. Eddie was my baby brother, eccentric, demanding, sometimes pretentious but unfailingly generous, and loving—a big teddy bear. I don't pretend to understand *why* my brother was gay. The truth is I don't *care* why. But, I do care that he died as he did *because* he was gay. I care that we didn't try to deal with this virus because it happened to affect homosexuals first. Gay men, innocent babies, unsuspecting wives of cheating husbands, whole populations in Africa are now paying the price of our dis-ease, our hesitation, our inaction in those early days—all because we thought it was okay to ignore homosexual persons.

If we don't allow immigrant children an education, the whole nation pays a price. If we don't improve wages for the working poor, it catches up with us. There is never a good reason to kill another, whether by withholding medical research or by administering lethal injection. It's as if we don't understand that, sooner or later, we all pay the price for the mistreatment.

In our Church, we can still hear the justification of intolerance when we are told that homosexuals are acceptable in the congregation but not as clergy. We hear some people in our church say that homosexuals are loved but their life-style is unacceptable. That's not love. We can "Tsk, tsk," assuming that all gay and lesbian persons have multiple partners. Then we can say that gay and lesbian couples shouldn't be intimate because they aren't married, and yet again have the audacity to keep them from exchanging vows at our altars.

The four corners of the world need to take up a part of the paralytic's pallet and place it at the feet of the only One who can help us out of our misery. If we are motivated by love, we can receive not only healing but forgiveness as well.

It isn't enough to find a way to stop AIDS. We have to be healed of hatred, bias, prejudice, and bigotry. The wounds caused by the AIDS virus are too deep for us to deal with effectively on our own. There will always be situations akin to AIDS around. We continue to find ways to hurt each other. And when we wound, we do it deeply. Only God's love can clean that putrid wound and heal it. Only God's forgiveness can make us whole again. It is no coincidence that Jesus' words to the paralytic are both healing and forgiveness. We need to ask for forgiveness early and often.

We have a better chance of getting through the crowd of issues and concerns if we, like the four friends of the paralytic, come together to seek healing and forgiveness from Jesus. And we will be more apt to stay together in the struggle if we are motivated by love. Love is the only thing that lasts, and love is the only way people change. We can't will them to change, and we can't talk them into change; we can only love them into change. Even justice and compassion fall short without the foundation of love to hold them up.

From the beginning of time, God's first act of love was creation. In the fullness of time, God came among us and dwelt with us to teach us about love and service. May we hold that truth in our hearts and minds, and may that truth guide our lives.

Sylvia Vasquez is associate rector for Latino ministry
at Trinity Church, Wilmington, Delaware.

GAY/LESBIAN RESPECT

Honoring an Alternative Story

Ruth 1:1–18
Dan Handschy

I WAS A little surprised to be asked to preach at this service. The church of which I am the rector undertook the Oasis discernment process this past spring. The congregation came to the verge of adopting the Affirmation of Welcome, then lost its nerve. The invitation to preach is a powerful testimony that the conversation Oasis seeks to initiate is not a coercive conversation, but a patient one. I wish to thank Oasis for recognizing the good but painful work we did in our discernment process. I honor Oasis for finding a way to continue to engage the whole church.

After the resolution asking for approval of forms for blessing same sex unions was defeated, none of the representatives of Integrity and other organizations working for full inclusion of gays and lesbians in the life of the church spoke of taking their marbles and going home. They were in the church for the long haul, they said, however slow that journey might be, however many tears they might have to shed along the way. How easy it would be to throw up one's hands in despair and go somewhere else! But they have all cast their lot with this Church.

The story told in the Book of Ruth is also about commitment to the long view, to a relationship over the course of time. Ruth is one of the most delightful books in the Bible, a touching, human story. Ruth's oath to her mother-in-law is compelling: "Do not ask me to forsake you. Wherever you go I will go, wherever you lodge I will lodge, your people shall be my people, your God my God. Wherever you die I will die, and there be buried. May the Lord do so to me and more besides, if aught but death separates me from you." Such human faithfulness moves us.

But the Book of Ruth is also a pointed social critique. You know how the story goes: Ruth returns with Naomi to Bethlehem, the city where David will be born. At Naomi's advice, Ruth gleans barley from the field of Boaz, a kinsman of Naomi's dead husband. Boaz tells the reapers to leave plenty for her to glean. Again, on Naomi's advice, Ruth goes out to the threshing floor at harvest time where Boaz is sleeping for the night, and says the Bible, "uncovers his feet to sleep there." Boaz wakes up and spreads his cloak over her.

This puzzled me until I learned that both "uncovering feet" and "spreading one's cloak" are Hebrew euphemisms for *sex*. Sex on the threshing floor was common in Canaan. It was a fertility rite in honor of Baal and Asherah, the fertility gods of Canaan before the time of the monarchies of Israel and Judah. Every planting time and harvest time, men and women had sex at the holy places (including the threshing floor) to assure the fertility of the land.

You know what happens after that. Boaz takes Ruth under his wing. He sends her home with six measures of barley. The next day he goes down to the city gate to see if Ruth has a closer relative than himself. She does, but he doesn't want to marry her and raise a family for Mahlon, Ruth's dead husband. Boaz acquires Naomi's field (really Elimelech's field) and marries Ruth to continue the line of Elimelech and Mahlon. Ruth gives birth to Obed. Obed becomes the father of Jesse, and Jesse becomes the father of David, the greatest monarch of Israel. It is a great story, but to get its point, we have to hear another story first.

You remember how the monarchy of David was divided after Solomon's death between the northern Kingdom of Israel and the southern Kingdom of Judah. Israel fell in the eighth century B.C.E. to the Assyrian Empire, and Judah fell in the sixth century B.C.E. to the Babylonian Empire. Many Judeans were carried off to Babylon in Exile. After fifty years in Babylon, at the rise of the Persian Empire, Darius the Persian allowed the Jews to return to Jerusalem and rebuild the Temple under the direction of Ezra the Scribe. The expectations of the returnees were seriously disappointed upon their arrival. Jerusalem was in ruins. The people living nearby had no apparent interest in reestablishing the YHWHistic cult. In fact, they were following the fertility practices of surrounding peoples. Ezra was none too happy. The ninth chapter of the Book of Ezra tells us that the leaders of the returnees approached Ezra with the report that "neither the Israelite laymen nor the priests nor the Levites have kept themselves aloof from the peoples of the land and their abominations (that is, the Canaanites, Hittites, Perizzites, Jebusites, Ammonites, Moabites [ah, the plot thickens— Ruth was a Moabite], Egyptians and Amorites); for they have taken some of their daughters as wives for themselves and their sons and thus they have desecrated the holy race with the peoples of the land."

Ezra tears his cloak and launches into a chapter long prayer of contrition. When he finishes, the leaders agree to take action. They covenant that all the people [read "men"] will "dismiss all our foreign wives and the children born of them, in keeping with what you, Ezra, advise." This tragic example of ethnic cleansing is found in our own Bible.

The Book of Ruth was written as a response to Ezra's policy. For all of its tender portrayal of Naomi, Ruth, and Boaz, the barb is very sharp. Sex at the threshing floor, a Canaanite fertility ritual, was one of the "abominations of the nations." In Ezra's day, Ruth, a Moabite woman, would have been sent packing, to become little better than a prostitute, if she were lucky enough to make it home. A Moabite woman, who had sex in a fertility ritual and married Boaz, a Jew, became the great grandmother of David. The Book of Ruth, therefore, subverts the ascendant viewpoint, calling ironically into question the prevailing orthodoxy of the day. The story is a much more cunning, delightful one than the triumphalist story told in Ezra and Nehemiah. Its inclusion in the canon asks the reader, "Which story would you rather have as your story?"

I believe the presence of gays and lesbians in our churches, seeking to tell their stories, serves for us like the Book of Ruth in the canon of Scripture, reminding us that there may be a more lovely story to be told than the story of the ascendant orthodoxy. And I believe that the counter-story being told by gays and lesbians in our midst is giving us another, healthier way of looking at human relationships, and particularly, sexual relationships.

The ascendant orthodoxy is that sex is only holy in the institution of marriage, and even then only with the possibility of procreation: the word used is *natural*. It seems to me that the mentality of shame clings to this view. It implies something of magic about the institution and form of marriage. Sex, not holy outside of marriage, suddenly becomes holy, after magic words are spoken by a magic personage. Something imbued with tremendous power to create but also to destroy must be hedged away from everyday life and kept in a safe place. Marriage, of course, also still carries vestiges of the notion of women as sexual property. Fathers still like to give away their daughters at their weddings. All this seems to come from the same impulse to hedge a force that changes persons and relationships in powerful ways. But we have left unexamined the assumptions that support the hedge.

"What happens when we bless a relationship?" When the church begins to ask the question, at the insistence of the gays and lesbians in our midst, a whole new discourse emerges. Covenanted, same-sex relationships are not about procreation. As such, they are not of keen interest to a society whose first concern is to replace its members. If same-sex relationships are to be holy, there will have to be some other reason. The discourse about blessing forces the church to disentangle its interests from the interests of the society at large. We are forced to ask the question, "What makes a relationship holy, rather than just expedient?"

Because of the stories of gays and lesbians at the edges of our canon, I believe the Church is discovering that we bless relationships because they are revelatory. Relationships that show us the nature of divine love are holy relationships. Relationships that encourage and allow partners to live into their full humanity, including their sexuality, relationships that guard the dignity of the partners, that enrich the lives of partners, reveal to us the nature of divine love.

Even more important, relationships the church can joyously bless are those that enrich the whole body of Christ. Among other things, Oasis is asking the church to enjoy the gifts that such relationships are ready to offer the church. When a couple, heterosexual, gay or lesbian, live together without benefit of blessing, the Body of Christ remains in some confusion about their status. Is this relationship about only the two of them? Is it only for their benefit? Do we share in its joys? Can we help carry their sorrows? Does it take priority over relationships to parents, friends, career? When the Church blesses a relationship, a marriage or a same-sex covenant, that relationship becomes part of the flesh of the Body of Christ. The Body is enriched by and has a stake in it. Seeing the partners sit together in church, embracing one another, rejoicing together, brings joy to the whole Body. Seeing the partners struggle through hard times brings grief to the whole Body, and the Body responds to help.

This discourse in the church is removing sex from the realm of taboo, and placing it in the realm of revelation. Sex becomes a sacramental sign of this particular revelatory relationship. The Church blesses this relationship so that it may reveal God's desire for the whole Body. The sacrament, the holy, is no longer to be found in the institutional form, supported by the legal apparatus of the society, with its remnants of taboo and property rights. Instead, the holy is found in the particular. *This* relationship is holy, revelatory, enriching the Body in a sacramental way. Even married people, because of this shift, need no longer understand themselves as constrained by the institutional form of marriage, but enriched by their sacramental participation in the whole life of the Body.

God is discovered not in the signature of a priest on a marriage license, but in the simple, daily things two people do to nourish, sustain, and enrich one another. God is found in putting a meal on the table, in doing laundry, in inviting friends to dinner, in back rubs, in flowers after a hard week at the office, in gardens, hobbies, leisure, and in the bedroom, where partners sustain and enrich one another sexually. People thus enriched and blessed can only enrich and bless the Church. Their lives together will a sign of the Realm of God.

Like Ruth's story, it may take a generation or two for the Church to incorporate this discourse into its way of thinking about God. But happen, it will.

I grew up in Colorado. Around my parents' house were many fields that were once farms, but had been left to go to weeds. Mustard was one of the first weeds to take over and one of the most tenacious. No one liked mustard, but you could see whole fields of yellow flowers in August. Jesus compares the Realm of God, where all humanity will live God's desires for them, to the seed of a mustard plant. Oasis is like a mustard seed. People may not want it around, may wish it would go away, but once it has established a foothold (as it has in the three congregations who have adopted the Statement of Welcome), it will not go away. People may wish this whole discourse about sex would just disappear; but here it is, like yeast in a lump of dough, that, in time, will raise the whole mass, making the bread much richer.

This is a marvelous beginning and a wonderful cause for celebration. However discouraging the work may be, remember the mustard seed. However foreign may seem the land where we sojourn, remember the story of Ruth. And however uncomfortable the conversation may be for the Church, we need to remember Naomi, Ruth, Boaz, Obed, Jesse, and

David. Oasis has done its part to enrich the story of the church and give us a story much lovelier than the ascendant orthodoxy. I hope the Church will take the time to hear this story and include it in our canon.

Dan Hanschy is rector of the Church of the Advent,
St. Louis, Missouri. The sermon was preached
at the Oasis Missouri Festival Eucharist.

EDUCATION

Dress for the Banquet!

Matthew 22:1–14
Proper 23 A
Anne S. Howard

HERE WE ARE, feeling good about all the outsiders gathered at the king's table. We can imagine the beggars from the road, the strangers, the widows and orphans, all the forgotten ones—this one from the shelter, that one from the group home, this one from the nursing home, that one from the street. All of them are welcome here, sitting in the place of princes, dining on the finest fare. The Gospel theme of inclusion wraps around this parable with a soft golden glow, with the warmth of, say, a *Big Fat Greek Wedding.*

But then, oops! The guest over there is wearing the wrong clothes! Usher him out! He didn't have the good sense to change into party clothes! Get him out of here! Forget all that about inclusion, about "come as you are," about "wherever you are in your journey of faith"; at this banquet in Matthew's Gospel, you have to wear the right outfit.

This is one of those times when the Bible includes something we might rather skip or just decide we don't like and re-interpret, according to our taste and values. This is one of those passages—there are many in the Bible—that we might like to edit out. If we could snip away at parts of the Bible we find offensive, we would end up with pages that look like a lace paper doily. But that kind of editing is a kind of fundamentalism—picking and choosing parts of the Bible to prove points to which one is pre-committed, going to Scripture as if it were an encyclopedia, looking for answers—our answers—to an issue. That's the kind of editing we attempt to do when we point to some parts of the Bible as coming from God and some parts coming from human authors.

An approach that affords more integrity to the text and to us as inheritors of Scripture is one that looks at the text in its setting as the human narrative of people trying to live in relation to God. We then ask two questions: "What did this text mean for the community who told it?" and "Why did they tell it this way?"

What did this mean to Matthew's community? Hearing this story, the community of Matthew recognized their own story, their predicament as first-century Jews separated from the temple worship in Jerusalem. They knew they were the outsiders, non-temple Jews. In their crowd were new converts, some Gentiles, who probably saw themselves as the ones invited in from the highways and byways to enjoy the feast that insiders, "observant Jews," had rejected. All these listeners might have heard about and celebrated the new radical inclusiveness of the Jesus movement. But why, then, tell the zinger about the wedding garment? Weren't they all welcome—like other parables said, like Jesus said—just as they were, no matter what their attire? Why this extra, second parable that doesn't appear in any of the other banquet parables?

Already the parable signals a change: look who is welcome at the feast. Not unusual for the new Jesus movement. But something more is going on here. The change goes beyond the invitation. The ones who couldn't be bothered to arrive in time for the feast failed to make the feast a priority. But the ones who failed to change, that is, to put on a new "garment," that symbol of a new way of living—they also missed out.

The Gospel of Matthew, full of instructions for the new first-century church, is reminding the community that life is different inside the Jesus movement, that even though everyone is welcome, much is expected. Coming to the feast means changing—changing priorities.

Matthew doesn't spell out the changes required. But the parable works to say: "Pay attention. Make a choice. This is not any banquet, this is life lived in a new way and it requires that you prepare, get ready, turn from whatever it is that occupies your mind, your time, your hands, and take on the work of this new kingdom, this kingdom devoted to including the least among us! This will not be business as usual. This will mean your priorities will change."

The two questions, "What did this parable, mean?" and "Why did they tell it this way?" help us get at the meaning for Matthew's community. The questions also help us see what lives for *us* in this text. What occupies the hours of our day? What preoccupies us in the middle of the night? What holds us? Matthew doesn't offer a neat recipe for change, a tidy list of things to do to get ready for a new life with God. None exists for us either, but the question remains: what are our priorities? What clothing might we change? The way of Jesus requires that we question how we live.

Some answers come from a modern-day teller of parables, a modern-day prophet who demands that we look to our priorities, a woman who has made it to the banquet and put on the wedding garment. Her name is Marian Wright Edelman, founder of The Children's Defense Fund, the organization set up to advocate for children's needs in this country, the organization that sponsors today's Children's Sabbath.

The daughter of a black Baptist preacher, Edelman has made it her life mission to speak up and speak out for children, especially for the eleven million poor children in our country. She backs up her conviction with numbers and facts that tell the story of these children. She makes it the business of the Children's Defense Fund to lobby Congress for the policy changes that mean a serious change in national priorities. Children must be our priority, she says, and tells the parable of the fifth child:

"Imagine a very wealthy family with five young children under the ages of three. Four have comfortable warm rooms in which to sleep. One does not. She lives in a cold room. Sometimes she has to sleep on the streets, or in a shelter. Imagine this family giving four of their children nourishing meals every day, but letting the fifth child go hungry. Imagine this wealthy family making sure four of their young children get all their shots and regular check-ups before they get sick, but ignoring the fifth child who is plagued by chronic infections in respiratory diseases like asthma. Imagine this rich family reading every night to their four children, but leaving the fifth child unread to, untalked and unsung to, or propped before a television screen which feeds her violence, ads for material things and intellectual pabulum."[1]

This parable, of course, is the parable of rich America, where one in five of our youngest children lives in poverty. "It is not a stable or strong or healthy family," Edelman says, "and it is not a sufficiently compassionate one."

Each year, as we make our annual observance of Children's Sabbath, we hear about our American family and the plight of our children. And this year, we know, our children face the plight of a new national setting of priorities, a setting of priorities that tells us our children will be safer and stronger and healthier only if we make a war in Iraq. Do we really believe that?

---

1. "Repairers of the Breach: Congregations Acting to Leave No Child Behind," 2002 Worship Resources Manual, Volume 11, published by the Children's Defense Fund.

What can we do? Why does the Children's Defense Fund call upon the people of faith in this country? As disciples of the Just One, what ought we to do? We can start in two places: with our government and with ourselves.

Several leaders in our nation have worked together to formulate new policy that gives priority to the needs of children. Last year The Act to Leave No Child Behind was introduced into Congress. It still serves as the standard to meet the needs of children in America, a standard much needed, as domestic legislation moves to the back burner in the face of war. This comprehensive legislation gives national, state, and local officials the opportunity to:

- Get every child ready for school through full funding of quality child-care, Head Start, and preschool programs.
- Ensure every child and their parents health insurance.
- Lift every child from poverty—half by 2004 and all by 2010.
- End child hunger through the expansion of food programs.
- Make sure every child can read by fourth grade and can graduate from school able to succeed at work and life.
- Provide every child safe, quality after-school and summer programs so children can learn, serve, work, and stay out of trouble.
- Ensure every child a place called home and decent affordable housing.
- Protect all children from neglect, abuse, and violence and ensure them the care they need.

This morning, the young people from our Rite 13 program have letters and envelopes ready for your signatures asking Lois Capps to cosponsor the Act. They also have information for you about the current national debate about war and the threat of terrorism and the range of responses available to us. And our Justice and Outreach Council has information about Trinity's involvement in after-school care at Casa de la Raza and the Children of Joy orphanage.

In our world, changing priorities means taking a stand for children, creating for them a world that is safe. Changing priorities means taking that stand on international, national, and personal levels. Your bulletin insert makes clear the plight facing children. Some simple ABCs offer some first steps toward solution. As always, the solution begins with one person. Somewhere near you a child asks for your love. Start small, start here, today: learn the name today of one child you don't know. But don't, *please don't,* just keep your love and your faith private. Take a few moments to learn what you can do as a citizen and person of faith—a citizen believer

(Martin Marty's term)—to challenge your government to care for the least among us. Be a citizen believer.

Join the banquet. See what that new garment might look like on you. The feast is ready right now. There's not a minute to waste.

Anne S. Howard is associate rector of Trinity Church,
Santa Barbara, California.

ECONOMIC INJUSTICE

Fire Burning in the Bones

Jeremiah 20: 7–18
Proper 7 A
Nancy Thurston

MY STOMACH has been churning since I realized that Jeremiah was the Scripture from which I would be preaching this morning. Jeremiah is a prophet of great passion whose words demand response. If I could have wiggled out of my commitment to preach today and still remained faithful to my call, I would have done it.

I understand Jeremiah's anguish. Early in his life, Jeremiah was drawn by God. He thought he was called to live a faithful life—decent and upstanding. Once God won his heart, however, the faithful life changed drastically. In today's passage he yells at God that he was tricked and overpowered against his will into a way of living that he neither expected nor wanted.

Jeremiah's bones burned. His heart writhed in pain. He was torn by love for God and love for his community. He was torn by the gap between God's call for honesty and justice for the poor, and the appalling behavior he was witnessing—behavior considered by most to be righteous and patriotic. He was torn by a call to utter harsh words he never wanted to speak. To the people he loved he spoke hard truth, unwelcome truth. He described them thus:

They judge not with justice the case of the fatherless. They do not defend the rights of the needy. Their tongue is a deadly arrow. It speaks deceitfully. With his mouth each speaks peaceably to his neighbors. But in his heart he plans an ambush for him.

I have always had a passion for following God. As a young adult I felt sure that I was to live a faithful life by being a bridge-builder, a nice, responsible teacher. My life focused on things I could get my hands around: family, community, charity to a few poor people near home, and, later, my physical therapy patients. Things outside that circle felt too big. I believed I couldn't really know the truth about hot topics of my day: Vietnam, Watergate, and Central American violence. Since these felt too big and the information was too confusing, I just ignored it all and left things in the hands of others.

Like Jeremiah, I was horrified to find that I, too, had been tricked by God. God overpowered me and called me into areas where I never wanted to go. Increasingly the "niceness" and "fitting in" that I so valued as a faithful person were forced to drop by the wayside as God shoved me onto this unexpected path. I was called to Haiti, where the boundaries of my heart were stretched almost to the breaking point. I found out, to my horror, that things I had heard years before about my beloved country's action in Latin America were things that actually *did* happen and were *still* happening in Haiti. I had to look at the direct link between my country's policies and the poverty and violence there.

We are leading an economic blockade against this poverty-stricken country under the guise of demanding elevated electoral and democratic standards. Haiti, an infant democracy, is obviously unable to attain these standards. At the same time, however, we do not press similar demands with far less democratic nations such as Saudi Arabia and China. Our tongue, in Haiti, is "a deadly arrow and we speak deceitfully," as America tries to undermine a democratically elected president who refuses to follow the structural adjustments that benefit wealthy countries and push poorer countries further into poverty.

Too often Jeremiah's words fit us: "With our mouth we speak peaceably to our neighbors, but in our heart we plan an ambush for them." I wish I knew more about other nations, but Haiti has become my window into seeing the direct connection between my lifestyle and that of my country, and the devastation of poorer countries around the world. All of the sudden, Jesus' central call toward people who are poor is no longer a matter of giving a few cans of food from my excess; it involves taking a stance as a Christian against what I see.

I don't want to know these things. I was much calmer, more satisfied not knowing—especially since the political changes of the last twenty-five years have financially benefited my family. It is hard to know what to do. My life is full of more and more paradoxes. I struggle with the fact that parts of my lifestyle still oppress the poor. That strange statement of Jesus, that I must lose my life in order to find it, is weaving its way into my experience. God tricked me into this knowledge as God tricked Jeremiah.

Christians lost a powerful opportunity for a prophetic witness last fall. One of the questions that arose after September 11 was, "Why do people hate us so much?" Americans were not willing to sit with that painful question long enough to hear the answer. That was bad enough. But when American Christians by and large refused also, that was a tragedy. Richard Rohr says that we cannot look full time at the world's suffering; we must turn away from time to time. But, he continues, if we refuse to look at all, we are complicit with evil. Right now, American Christians are on a dangerous path by letting nationalism and patriotism take the front seat and letting our nation, rather than our faith, set the questions we are willing to ask and the answers we are willing to explore.

When I walked into this sanctuary a few weeks ago and saw the American flag up front, the fire in my bones almost consumed me. I know that the flag stands for so much more than what we are doing as a nation right now, for so much more than our refusal to see things from any perspective other than our own. But right now, Christians have an important alternative to live in the world. Last fall Bishop Gregg said that Christians were to be people of reconciliation. That is true. To get there we must sit with that painful question, "Why do people hate us so much?" There are many answers, all of which are very hard to hear and which demand a response from us as a country, as individuals, and especially as Christians. We can continue to turn away and ignore this question only at deep peril to our relationship to God.

It is normal to assume that we can live as Christians merely by being decent folks. Jeremiah thought so. I thought so. Millions have thought so. But it is not true. The Gospel offers a drastic alternative to our nation's approach, to any nation's approach. The time to wake up has come.

As Christians our family includes the global family, not just our immediate family. As Christians, homeland security must be worldwide homeland security. Jeremiah reminds us that God "delivered the life of the needy from the hands of evildoers." As Christians the welfare of the needy is as important as the welfare of our own children. We can't support a system that starves and endangers some children so that ours will have overflowing plates and unlimited opportunities.

I didn't want to say this. I wish Jeremiah would return and call us to repentance. But today, with fear and trembling, with a fire burning in my bones, I can no longer remain silent. God tricked me, and I cannot ignore or backpeddle anymore.

Jeremiah knew both anger at this life of faith and a sense of deep connection with God. Many Christians today and in times past have walked this narrow road. It looks impossible and, without God's help, it is impossible. But the choice is to say yes to this Gospel way or walk away. And the time for response is *now!* God's people and God's earth are being destroyed while we sit back unquestioning.

Are we willing to reject this amazing gift because we fear the weight of the burden?

Nancy Thurston is rector of St. Paul's Church, Klamath Falls, Oregon.

FOREIGN POLICY

Risks in Speaking Out—Or Not

Jeremiah 15:15–21; Matthew 16:21–27
Proper 17 A
Susan Thon Burns

JUST THE other day, I was sitting outside under a tree in the backyard at the bay enjoying the unaccustomed cool weather and gentle breeze, when the words of a song I learned years ago at summer camp came into my head. "And every man 'neath his vine and fig tree shall live in peace and unafraid." Our house at the bay is not big or fancy. It is in a neighborhood of modest houses, set close together, with small yards, front and back. As I sat there with the song singing away in my head, I decided that the neighborhood really has the feel of each one under his vine and fig tree, living in peace and unafraid.

I remembered that these ancient words had floated up at other times recently, in quiet moments, in the background, behind the turmoil, danger, violence, and deep sadness of the world's events. That, I thought, is really my vision of peace, my understanding of God's desire for the world: that all the nations, all the peoples, each and every person can have a vine, a fig tree, a place to live in peace and unafraid.

Yet how impossible it seems right now for even this small vision to be realized for so many of the world's people! How difficult it is, and always has been, to speak out about even so small and simple a vision of good, of a level of well-being for each person, of a just society, a just world, and of peace. The conversations so quickly become so complex, so confrontational and polarized. For even so small a vision of good to be realized, so many competing interests come into play.

The prophets preached about God's desire for a just society and peace. Just look at the trouble it brought them! That is much of what Jesus himself did, because while he was not *only* a prophet, he *was* a prophet. And what that brought him was great suffering and death.

The words of the camp song come from the prophet Micah, who predicted the fall of Jerusalem in the eighth century B.C.E. because of the corruption of its rulers. It was Micah who gave us these words: "And what does the Lord require of you but to do justice, and to love kindness, and to walk humbly with your God?" Micah also foresaw that in the time of God's justice, "they shall beat their swords into plowshares, and their spears into pruning hooks; nation shall not lift up sword against nation, neither shall they learn war any more."

But much as people may have treasured these words down the ages since, Micah was not popular in his own day, because the truth he spoke was not what people wanted to hear. They did not want to hear that the Assyrians would overrun Jerusalem as they already had overpowered Samaria. They wanted to hear that the security and prosperity of Jerusalem would continue undisturbed. "Do not preach . . . one should not preach of such things; disgrace will not overtake us," the official state prophets said to Micah when he said that Jerusalem would fall because of the injustice and oppression in her society.

A century later, Jeremiah also found that to be a prophet was a painful calling. He spoke out of conscience about the dangers he foresaw for his people. Assyria *had* conquered Jerusalem, as Micah foresaw, but Assyria's control over Jerusalem and the land of Judah was ending by Jeremiah's day. The people were optimistic about their new situation. They were convinced that it proved they were Yahweh's chosen people. Many believed that Yahweh would protect them now, no matter what.

Jeremiah, though, saw that it *did* matter how Judah conducted its affairs, and how its people lived. He warned that an even great disaster lay on the horizon for his nation. For forty years he was mocked and called a fool because he condemned a way of life that people and their leaders found comfortable—until Judah *was* conquered by Babylon and carried off into exile.

Mostly during those forty years, no one listened to Jeremiah. He had thought that, if he was faithful to the truth and preached what the Lord told him to say, the people would listen and change their lives. But they did not listen, and he became a laughingstock. When the religious leadership did listen, they had Jeremiah arrested, beaten, and put in the stocks at the gate of the temple. What a painful life! What are we to make of it?

Jesus also knew what it was *not* to be heard, *not* to be understood. He knew what it meant to meet with opposition and rejection. Like the prophets before him, he might, at times, have been tempted to tell the people what they wanted to hear, or at least to water down the message a little—making it easier to swallow, more acceptable to the people.

Even his closest follower, Peter, the one who recognized him for who he really was, "The Christ, the Son of the living God," urged him to take another way, not the way to Jerusalem, to suffering and death. *Do what it takes to save your life*, Peter pleaded. And it's no surprise, really, that Jesus turned on Peter at that point and called him "Satan." "Get behind me, Satan! You are a stumbling block to me." In effect, he was saying to Peter, "You are thinking not as God does, but as human beings do."

The temptation to do things his own way, a safer, more comfortable way, instead of God's way, was the same temptation that Satan, the Tempter, had presented to Jesus in the wilderness after his baptism.

Then Jesus turned to all his disciples and said, "If any want to become my followers, let them deny themselves and take up their cross and follow me. For those who want to save their life will lose it, and those who lose their life for my sake will find it. For what will it profit them if they gain the whole world but forfeit their life?"

We know these words are meant for us, as followers of Jesus. But there are some difficulties as we think about what it means to live this out. For one thing, we are painfully aware now, if we were not before, that terrible, violent, destructive acts have been done, and vicious, violent words spoken, by people who believed they were following the will of God and were willing to give up their lives to do it. I am thinking not only of the men who crashed airplanes into buildings on September 11, killing themselves, the passengers, and more than three thousand innocent people (though I *am* thinking of those men). And I am thinking of the suicide bombers in Israel. But I am thinking also of some of our own Christian forbears, just as militant and sectarian as any militant religious fanatics today.

For example, there was Bernard of Clairvaux, a saint of the Church, the founder of the Cistercian monastic order, a giant figure in Christianity. Bernard of Clairvaux campaigned for a Second Crusade to free Jerusalem from the Muslims in the twelfth century. He wrote a pamphlet for the Knights Templars. That pamphlet includes these thoughts: "The soldiers of Christ do not know the least fear, neither for sin, when they kill their enemies, nor for danger that they themselves might perish. This is because to kill someone for the sake of Christ, to risk death, is not only completely free of sin, but highly praiseworthy."[1]

---

1. "Praise of the New Knighthood," quoted in John W. Kiser, *The Monks of Tibhirine* (New York: St. Martin's Press, 2002), 78.

We are *right* to be leery of any words we might feel inspired to speak in God's name or on God's behalf that might lead to violence toward another person or might take another person's dignity or humanity. But this caution, this recognition that people have done and will do terrible things out of religious conviction, does not let us off the hook. We don't have the option of not speaking or acting out of conscience and religious conviction just because it is risky, in more ways than one.

In the September 2002 issue of *Episcopal Life*, the Presiding Bishop, The Right Reverend Frank Griswold, had some relevant thoughts on this question. There *is* a risk, a temptation to assume, as Bishop Griswold points out, that "my concerns and my perspectives match those of God." At the same time, though, there is still the imperative to examine our personal, communal, and national life "in the light of the deep values we draw from Scripture and our life in Christ, which reveal to us something of God's desires and intentions."[2]

If we are trying to be faithful to the values we draw from Scripture and our life in Christ, we are bound to find ourselves raising questions in sensitive areas, sometimes difficult and painful questions. And this is a second difficulty I see as I try to obey Jesus' command to deny oneself and take up the cross and follow him. I mean, what do we do with our questions once we see them? If we have questions, for example, about our country's continued and significant aid to Israel, in light of Israel's policies toward the Palestinians, how, where, and with whom do we raise them? How openly can we talk about them in the church? What is the risk to your relationships with your Jewish friends and neighbors if you explore your questions too deeply? What is the risk to your relationships with Muslim friends and neighbors if you raise questions about the Palestinians' policies and actions? Telling the truth, even trying to discern what the truth is, is risky.

Another example is the beginning debate about our country's policy toward Iraq. Why is it so urgent *now* to change that country's leadership, and by military means? Is there new or newly discovered evidence that Iraq has made a significant advance in development of some weapon of mass destruction? That it is moving toward using its weapons against us, or our allies, or giving them to some group that will? Have the pursuit of terrorists and military action in Afghanistan presented an opportunity to invade Iraq, because the American Congress and public would support such

---

2. Frank Griswold, "One Year Later Continuing to Make Meaning," *Episcopal Life* Column, September 2002.

an invasion of Iraq now, while they might not have before September 11 of last year?

Just suggesting those questions here today creates a risk, that some of you may not think it is appropriate to raise questions about politics and national policy in church, especially from the pulpit. I can't help but be aware of that. And I also can't help but be aware of the position of the prophets of Israel and Judah, who found that trying to be faithful and listen to God often put them right in the middle of questions about politics and national policy.

Bishop Griswold wrote, "To live under God requires a conversion of heart and a willingness to see things not solely from the perspective of self-interest but from the perspective of God's universal care for the well-being of all people and the creation that sustains us." How do we, as Christians, come to see issues not only from the perspective of our own self-interest, but also from the much broader perspective of God's care for all people and all creation? Can we have the conversations and ask the questions that will help all of us gain that broader perspective, based in our reading of Scripture and our life in Christ, even as we recognize that we will not always agree?

There is risk in that, but there is also risk in avoiding it. There always has been. Just ask Jeremiah, who suffered because he asked questions and spoke about what he saw; but who also said that if he did not speak out, the word became like a burning fire shut up in his bones. Or ask Jesus, who said that always playing it safe may lose you your soul.

There is a story told about a man named Ammon Hennacy, who was part of the Catholic Worker movement and a friend of its founder, Dorothy Day. Once in the 1960s, Hennacy was in South Dakota, in the dead of winter, protesting at a missile silo. There were just a handful of other protesters with him, two soldiers behind a fence, and one local reporter. That was it. The wind was blowing, and it was below freezing, which just served to highlight how pointless the protest seemed to be. After about twenty minutes, the reporter walked over to Hennacy and shouted into the wind, "Do you really think you're going to change the government by being out here?" Hennacy replied, "My friend, I'm out here so that the government doesn't change *me*."[3]

Which is not to imply, that any of us necessarily should have been, or should now be, protesting at missile silos or missile transport trains. But it *is* to say that following Christ must sometime lead us to some words or

---

3. As told by Jim Barnett, OP, in "First Impressions" 22nd Sunday in Ordinary Time (A), September 1, 2002, from jboll@mindspring.com.

acts of conscience and commitment, be they words or acts of kindness, charity, generosity, protest, or prophecy. Something that, even though it may put us at risk, will save us in the end, because it contributes to God's vision of peace and well-being, when every man 'neath his vine and fig tree shall live in peace and unafraid. And which is also to say that this *is* the place for us to discern together how we are—and each one of us is— called to find the words and the actions that will help in some small way to bring about that dream of God.

Susan Thon Burns is rector of The Church of the Redeemer, Bethesda, Maryland.

TERRORISM

Coming to Terms with Being Lost

1 Timothy 1:12–17; Luke 15:1–10
Proper 19 C
Anthony Moon

IT WAS nearing lunch time. I was in kindergarten. Suddenly it dawned on me that my two older brothers had brought their lunches but I had not. I found my brothers on the playground with their brown bags in hand. I didn't have any lunch, I told them, and I didn't know what to do. Could they share some of their lunch, or should I go home? We had walked that eight-block trek every day to and from school, but I had not traveled it many times by then, and I'd never walked it by myself. In the wisdom of a second grader and an eight grader, it must have been an easy answer: "Just walk home for lunch." I started out from the familiar sur-roundings of our grade school. Mid-way, and with each passing step, the homes and the street and the sidewalks took on an unfamiliar quality. I wasn't sure anymore that this was the right way home. I walked on, not even thinking of turning back. The notion that I was lost was dawning in my mind. Finally, I had to admit it: I *was* lost. No sooner had I admitted the truth to myself, it seemed, than I heard a familiar voice: "Hey, boy! Need a ride?" I turned to see my dad's old red pickup truck and his smil-ing face. I jumped in the truck and we were off. My father rescued me from a fate of who-knows-what.

Today's readings focus on being lost and being found. St. Paul writes that he was once lost: "I was a blasphemer, a persecutor, a man of violence." He goes on to describe how he was found: "I had acted ignorantly in unbelief, and the grace of our Lord overflowed for me with the faith and love that are in Christ Jesus . . . Christ Jesus came into the world to save sinners—of whom I am the foremost. But for that very reason I received mercy," St. Paul says.

In the Gospel, Jesus is scorned by the Pharisees as one who welcomes sinners and eats with them. In reply, Jesus offers two parables of loss. He asks: "What shepherd who loses one sheep will not leave his ninety-nine other sheep to find the lost one. When the one sheep is found, the shepherd rejoices, calling together his friends and neighbors to rejoice with him. What woman with ten silver coins, losing one of them, does not light a lamp, sweep her house and carefully search until she finds the lost one. When found, will she not also call her friends and relatives to rejoice in finding the lost coin?" Jesus knows that God and his angels will rejoice in the repentance of one sinner.

In light of this week's events, we know that there are many, many lost people. Rescuers have been working non-stop at an overwhelming task to find those lost in the wreckage of the collapsed World Trade Center and the Pentagon. There has been round-the-clock media coverage. People have engaged in many conversations, trying to understand what has happened, and trying to think about what the weeks ahead will bring. In New York City, in our nation, and in the world, there has been shock, disbelief, anger, frustration, and tears. And, here in the heart of Oklahoma, many have re-lived the events of an April day in 1995.

Beyond those lost in the wreckage, many of us across the nation and around the world are lost in disbelief, outrage, anger. Observing the e-mail commentaries that have come my way this week, the newspaper and media coverage, and the conversations, I see a natural reaction to such an atrocity. Fear and attack: "We will hurt you like you have hurt us. And then some. We shall seek revenge. An eye for an eye." Hatred is alive and well.

Two years ago this week, Marian and I and several others from this parish were in England on a tour of ancient Anglican cathedrals. One of the most arresting sites we encountered was at Coventry Cathedral, a cathedral bombed during World War II. We were awestruck by the devastation we beheld, but we were even more awestruck by the story related by our guide.

On a Saturday evening during World War II, German bombers flew over the city of Coventry and unleashed their bombs. The city was ripped open, bomb by bomb. One casualty of the attack was Coventry Cathedral. All that remained were a few walls containing shattered rubble.

The rubble long cleared away, our tour group stood staring at the open sky where a roof should be, when our guide told us that the morning after the bombing, Sunday morning, the priest and other survivors of the parish came together to worship and to see the devastation of their cathedral. At the service of worship, this congregation decided to dedicate themselves to forgiving their attackers. On that day, they decided to make forgiveness a prominent part of their community identity and a cornerstone of their move forward, of their healing. Word of this brave stance spread. They eventually built another cathedral adjoining the wreckage, which they left as a testament and a reminder of their path to forgiveness and healing. The new cathedral now has tall stained glass windows given by Germany in acknowledgement of the congregation's forgiveness.

So besides those of us who are lost today in our feelings and fears, who else is lost? Our attackers. Whatever shape our response to this atrocity takes, it can only be driven either by fear or by love. We know that on many occasions, Jesus commanded his followers to "fear not." We also know that as followers of Christ, we are commanded to "love one another as we love ourselves."

What I am asking us to do is to temper our thinking and our words to those of *justice*, and not give in to revenge. Through justice, misguided actions can be thoughtfully judged and a suitable consequence established. In the overwhelming evidence of this tragedy, I know that justice may be a difficult thing to wrap our minds around. Revenge is much easier. I also know that these words may be difficult for some to hear. A disbelieving part of me finds them equally hard to say. "Maybe the timing is not right," I thought while preparing this sermon. "Maybe in a week or two, we could talk about forgiveness and justice."

But, just as our English friends at Coventry came to grips with their destruction, I believe we too must also come to a Christian conclusion as well. It is in this very crisis that we must now respond with love and compassion for all of God's children.

In the weeks to come there will be many conversations into which we will enter, in which we will be asked to give our opinion. We must consider the effects of what we say as adding to an awakening of Christ's consciousness or merely promoting the hatred of the world. We must consider that our beliefs, our words, and our actions will either lead to our healing or will lead to our demise.

And though we might not find him in an old red pickup truck, perhaps when we admit that we are lost, we can begin to search for the welcoming face of our Father. As we pray for the victims of violence, let us also pray for the courage to forgive. Pray for peace. Pray for healing.

Anthony Moon is deacon at St. Mary's Church, Edmond, Oklahoma.

DESCRIBING DIMENSIONS
OF PROPHETIC SPEECH

Welcoming Prophets—Receiving Their Rewards

Jeremiah 28:5–9; Matthew 10:40–42
Proper 8 A
Mariann Edgar Budde

ON A HOT day like today, we can appreciate the value of a cold cup of water, and why such hospitality might be so lavishly rewarded. I'm not sure what Jesus meant, however, when he said that whoever welcomes a prophet receives a prophet's reward. Prophecy isn't, in general, a rewarding vocation. All that a prophet can reasonably expect this side of heaven is grief and frustration. Thus, if we are to welcome a prophet and the prophet's message, we should prepare ourselves to receive something of the same.

It's not hard to figure out why prophets are not welcome in their own town, among their own people (as Jesus himself said in another context). God calls prophets for one reason: to speak a truth that no one else can hear. Or perhaps, more accurately, to speak the truth that everyone else more or less knows, but chooses not to face. To see and hear what everyone else also sees and hears but chooses to push outside the realm of consciousness and responsibility.

Think of how, as individuals, we respond when someone insists on speaking a truth that we have been avoiding. Rarely do we say, "Thank you for pointing that out to me." Multiply that denial, resistance, and even anger to the level of an entire society, and you get a sense of what prophets are up against. "Whoever welcomes a prophet receives a prophet's reward." To paraphrase St. Teresa of Avila, "If that's how God's friends are treated, maybe that's why God has so few of them."

What reward might there be in speaking and living difficult, costly truth? Or what motivation is there to do so when, quite honestly, there seems to be no reward at all? What incentive might we have to welcome a prophet and to bear the cost of that association, when in the short term we gain nothing?

Most prophets, truth be told, speak with great reluctance. Certainly that was the case with the prophet Jeremiah. Jeremiah was called to his vocation at a most difficult time. His world, as biblical scholar Water Brueggemann writes, "was literally coming unglued, by internal neglect and abdication, moral cynicism among the powerful and by external threat. Most astonishing is that while this was going on, nobody noticed."[1]

No one wanted to deal with the reality crashing in on the nation. Rulers and prophets alike assured themselves and the people that all would be fine. Jeremiah knew better. Jeremiah not only saw what was happening, he had a sense of why it was happening and of what God was going to do to save Israel—*which was nothing at all*. God was not going to spare them from destruction this time. God, Jeremiah knew, was going to let the unthinkable happen. He didn't want to say this. He preferred not to speak, but it was as if he had no choice, as if the truth would kill him if he kept it to himself.

That's how it is with most prophets, I think, for there is no satisfaction in being right about hard things. Yet the truth is so powerful that prophets feel compelled to speak and live with its implications, even in the face of resistance and anger. Perhaps we welcome the prophet's word only when we, too, have been convicted by truth.

The other great motivation for prophets is love. They risk speaking truth out of love for those around them and a deep desire for things to be better. Jeremiah's reaction to Hananiah, the other prophet mentioned in today's text, illustrates this point. Picture the scene: the nation has been overrun; the political and spiritual leadership has been sent into exile. Hananiah, a prophet of the king, presumably speaking for God, assures the nation that the Babylonian occupation will be short. There is no need to worry, no need to make drastic adjustments. God will provide. Peace and prosperity will return shortly.

Jeremiah is stunned by Hananiah's words, for it is the opposite of what he himself has heard from God—that the occupation and exile will be long and that the people must learn the spiritual lessons of hardship. But what Jeremiah says is, "Amen! May the Lord fulfill the words you have spoken."

Jeremiah *prefers* Hananiah's prophecy to his own, because he loves his people. He wishes that he himself were wrong and Hananiah right, so that the people would be spared. But, Jeremiah concludes, only time will tell. "If your words of peace come true, then we'll know that you are speaking for the Lord."

As it turned out, Jeremiah was right and Hananiah was wrong, which is one reason Jeremiah has a book in the Bible and Hananiah doesn't. Hananiah

---

1. Walter Brueggemann, *The Threat of Life* (Minneapolis: Augsburg Press, 1996), 72.

told people what they wanted to hear, but he lied. Jeremiah spoke truth in love, although the people didn't like what he had to say. Yet he bore their resentment and spoke anyway, out of love. When we welcome the prophet's words, it is out of love that we must do so, taking no pleasure in being right, willing to bear the burden of rejection for the sake of greater good.

Who might be the prophets of our time that Jesus asks us to welcome? Who are the ones speaking the truths we know but as a people are not yet ready to face? It's not easy to tell sometimes. We know the prophets of the past, even our not-so-distant past, because we now accept the truth of what they were trying to tell us. We name streets and schools after our past prophets—Martin Luther King, of course, and Rosa Parks, Susan B. Anthony, Harriet Tubman. But at the time of their struggles, life was much more difficult for these people, as well as for those who welcomed them. Witnessing to the truth often requires a high price before the tide turns toward more universal acceptance.

Here's one story: inside the National Cathedral of Washington, D.C., there are flags from all states in the union, each representing significant people from those states. Georgia has three flags—one for Martin Luther King, one for Woodrow Wilson, and one for Robert Alston.

Who was Robert Alston? A member of the Georgia legislature determined to reform it during a time of heinous corruption. He was particularly offended by the practice of loaning state prisoners to wealthy and influential people to work on their mansions, build their buildings, or farm their plantations. Prisoners who worked all day for no pay built many of the finest buildings in Atlanta. "It's worse than slavery," Alston said, but no one else seemed interested. His colleagues didn't want to disrupt a system of which they were the beneficiaries. The more he spoke up, the more he was ostracized by his peers.

One day Alston announced that he was introducing legislation to stop the abuse of prison labor. The next day a fellow legislator shot him dead. To speak and act on what he knew to be true cost him his life. Eventually the abuse stopped, in no small measure because of the price Alston paid. And now Georgia flies a flag in his honor.[2]

Who are the prophets now? Who are speaking the truths we wish to avoid but that our children's children will accept as obvious? In whose name will future monuments be built? What price would there be for welcoming a prophet of today and taking our share of the resistance and reaction to truth?

There is a lot of truth-telling going on in American business and on Wall Street these days, ugly truth that it seems at last we are ready to hear. And

---

2. As told by Fred Craddock in his sermon, "Why the Cross?" found in *The Cherry Log Sermons* (Louisville: Westminster/John Knox Press, 2001), 81.

while we are right to be outraged by the gross excesses and the doctoring of financial records to maintain the illusion of growth, it's important to remember that, amid the financial frenzy of the last decade, we all knew that things weren't right. We didn't want to talk much about it, as our own portfolios were increasing. We didn't question CEO salaries when stock prices were high. And when some courageous souls dared to question a company's sales or profits, they were ignored or even shouted down by other shareholders. Who is speaking truth now about the health of our financial institutions, now that we're beginning to listen, and what would it cost us to accept it?

There is considerable truth-telling in the scientific community now, with a growing consensus among scientists around the world about the impact of human consumption and pollution on our planet. We are destroying habitat at an alarming rate, leaving future generations at risk, and we know it. Yet we continue on with an unsustainable way of life, with a government refusing to participate in international efforts to reduce pollution levels. We even have our "court prophets," scientists willing to tell us what we want to hear, that things aren't as bad as others claim. Maybe so, but the future costs of doing nothing now are enormous. How might welcoming a prophet's word about the risks to our planet change the way we ourselves live on it?

In the Middle East, there are prophetic voices on both sides—courageous Israelis daring to speak out against the onslaught of violence against whole villages and against Jewish settlements in the occupied territory, which are as offensive to Palestinians as suicide bombers are to Israelis. There are Palestinians willing to speak out publicly against the suicide bombings, willing to say that even though the United States has placed on them the initial burden of reform (wrongly, I believe, in its imbalance), their government *is* in need of reform that must be addressed.

In this country there are those who remind us that we are not innocent bystanders, with our military support and abdication of global responsibility. Everyone knows what needs to happen for peace. Everyone knows. The only unknown is how many more lives will be lost before peace is sought. How many more lives must be lost before we do what we all know needs to be done?

In the churches, controversy rages on about the rightful place for gay and lesbian Christians—thankfully not in this congregation, but elsewhere, fueled by ignorance and prejudice veiled as theology. Are we willing to proclaim with courage the truth that we live? It's not difficult to speak about gay/lesbian inclusion in this parish anymore, although it was at one time. It's harder in the broader councils of the church that are more polarized, where the stakes are higher. It isn't easy to speak the truth that we know.

It isn't easy to listen, either, to receive a prophetic word when there are so many voices clamoring for our attention and conflicting messages in the name of God. Some of us are reading Bishop Spong's latest book, *A New Christianity for a New World*, which is his self-conscious prophetic attempt to rescue the Christian faith from fundamentalism and an outdated worldview and understanding of God. Others are seeking to rescue the church from Bishop Spong! How are we to distinguish among those claiming truth? Perhaps more important, how are we to trust our own instincts, after we've realized how easily we can be deceived or lulled into easy truths or kept quiet by our fear of controversy?

Jesus gives us a place to begin when he speaks of hospitality—welcoming the prophet, welcoming the righteous person, welcoming a child. A cold cup of water goes a long way and so does an internal willingness to consider challenging viewpoints, perspectives that are not our own, or truths that are difficult to hear. If the only prophets I receive are those I agree with, I have not yet learned hospitality. What I listen for, in others and in myself, is the passion of conviction that can propel us past what makes us uneasy to the place of truth. What I look for, in others and in myself, is speech and action motivated by love rather than self-righteousness, the willingness to risk rejection out of concern for what is best.

That may be the prophet's reward Jesus talks about: Truth so compelling that we have no choice but to stand by it. Love so deep that we are willing to risk all for it. Knowledge that what we are striving for is of ultimate significance. With such rewards, we would no longer need to make much of that which matters little, no longer miss the opportunity to participate in the greatest challenges of our time.

We will be judged, if not by God, surely by future generations, who will ask us, "Where were you and what were you doing in the time of struggle for truth?"

Mariann Edgar Budde is rector of St. John the Baptist Church, Minneapolis, Minnesota.

Re-Naming Reality as Scriptural Sabbath

Luke 4:14–21
Judith M. McDaniel

JESUS IS a preacher. This morning Jesus not only tells us three times that he is a preacher, he also enacts that fact: Jesus comes to Nazareth, where he was brought up, and goes to the synagogue on the Sabbath day, as is his custom. He stands up to read, and the scroll of the prophet Isaiah is given to him. He unrolls the scroll and finds the place where it is written: "The Lord . . . has sent me as a herald of joy . . . to preach release . . . to preach a year of the Lord's favor." Then he interprets: "Today this scripture has been fulfilled in your hearing." Armed with the power of the Spirit, Jesus yanks his listeners into another reality, a realm that is truer than anything they have ever known before. He causes them to see their world with new eyes. Jesus is a preacher.

There's our assignment, preachers: The ministry inaugurated at Nazareth is, after all, the paradigm for your ministry and mine. So, go. Go to your home congregation on Sundays, as is your custom. Go as a herald . . . of good tidings. Preach . . . of a world released from the captivity of lesser gods. Proclaim . . . a time of the Lord's favor, a time when all life is seen from the perspective of God's vision. Broadcast the news . . . that the Scripture is being fulfilled in our hearing. Can you and I make that claim? Can we wrench our listeners into another reality, a realm that is truer than anything they have ever known before? Are we armed with the Spirit or otherwise armed? Do we dare to re-describe reality, to tell the way things are in God's eyes and invite our listeners to adjust their vision to see the world from the Bible's perspective? Standing in the shadows of war and snipers, do we dare to preach?

Jesus is a preacher, an expository preacher. The year of the Lord's favor is not a topic Jesus superimposes upon just any biblical text. Neither does he survey the ever-present structures of poverty, oppression, and intolerance, then search for a biblical passage that can be used as a prooftext to address those needs. No, Jesus respects the integrity of the text. He exegetes the scroll given to him.

So, one might ask, what did you hear? There is no mistaking *his* thesis. We hear themes of Jubilee, the re-ordering of relationships, themes that pervade Hebrew scripture.

When those in the synagogue heard Jesus read from Isaiah 61:1–2, they heard echoes of Isaiah 58:6 and allusions to Exodus [21:2–6], Leviticus [25:10ff], Deuteronomy [15:1–18], Nehemiah [5:1–13], and Jeremiah [34:13–22]. All the proclamations of Sabbath year laws found in Exodus and Deuteronomy, and royal decrees of amnesty and release found in Jeremiah and Nehemiah, come together in Leviticus [25:10ff] and lend significance to Jesus' interpretation of Isaiah. The development and connotations of these passages are diverse, but all affirm God's sovereign mandate of deeds of justice and liberation. All would echo in the minds of Jesus' listeners. Jesus took seriously the demands and promises of the Hebrew Scriptures, and he used those Scriptures as a lens through which to view the demands and promises of his culture. He dared to look at his culture from the perspective of God's vision for that civilization. Jesus was a preacher.

There's our assignment preachers: to take seriously the demands and promises of Scripture and preach to a culture under the captivity of lesser gods. If we are to preach the re-ordering of relationships to this culture, we cannot ignore the resonances of Scripture's call for justice and liberation. Themes of the redistribution of power are pervasive in Scripture. The New Testament echoes the Old. Any New Testament passage that speaks of righteousness and release is on a trajectory that began in the Old Testament. That trajectory began with the demand for מְשְׁפַּט, justice and ends in the New Testament with the promise of δικαιοσυνη, right relationship.

Nor will we treat the Old Testament as less authoritative than the New. We have all heard sermons that flee to the New Testament for answers to the issues raised in the Hebrew Scriptures. We have heard Bultmann's claim that Israel's God is not our God! But Jesus does not make such a claim. The Hebrew Scriptures were Jesus' holy book. The God of Israel was Jesus' holy father. Jesus "belongs to the world of the Old Testament."[1] He is the link between the two testaments. So the first principle of preaching to be derived from Jesus' use of Scripture is to take seriously the Old Testament, both its demands and its promises, and to use both testaments as a lens through which to see our culture from the perspective of God's vision. Do we dare?

Jesus was a preacher. When Jesus preached, his listeners heard Jubilee language, language with which they were familiar; but they also heard something deeper. They heard the commandments that stand at the very heart of the message of Deuteronomy [6:4ff]. They heard what Patrick Miller[2] calls the "sabbatic principle." The sabbatic principle permeates biblical ethics. The sabbatic principle does *not* mean "take a little time off from work or study to recharge your batteries." The sabbatic principle means that the Sabbath is the basis of all relationships. If Jubilee is about the restoration of right relationship, the Sabbath is the basis of that restoration. Jesus went to the synagogue on the Sabbath as was his custom and proclaimed a year of release and restoration that is simply an extension of the basic Sabbath command.

---

1. Sidney Greidanus, *Preaching Christ from the Old Testament: A Contemporary Hermeneutical Method* (Grand Rapids, Michigan: William B. Eerdmans, 1999), 49.

2. Patrick D. Miller, *Deuteronomy* (Interpretation; Louisville: Westminster/John Knox Press, 1990), 134–40, and "The Human Sabbath: A Study in Deuteronomic Theology," *Princeton Theological Seminary Bulletin* 6 (1985), 81–97.

In his book , *The Sabbath*[3], Abraham Joshua Heschel tells the following Rabbinic legend:

At the same time when God was giving the Torah to Israel, he said to them, "My children, if you accept the Torah, and observe my commandments, I will give you for all eternity a thing most precious that I have in my possession." "And what," asked Israel, "is that precious thing which thou wilt give us if we obey thy Torah?" "The world to come—the world to come," said the Lord. "Show us in this world an example of the world to come, [said] Israel. "The Sabbath—the Sabbath is an example of the world to come. . . ." replied God.

The Sabbath is an example of the world to come, a realm in which the world and human relationships are restored to their created character and intention,[4] a realm that is truer than anything we have ever known before.

The command to keep Sabbath is second only to the *Shema*. If the primary purpose of human existence is whole-hearted and total worship and obedience of God—you shall love the Lord your God with all your heart, and with all your soul, and with all your mind—then keeping the Sabbath follows; for it takes time to develop a relationship. Proper balance and relationship in union with God and one another require Sabbath time when all creation is restored to a deeper level of rest and reflection. Sabbath is when the world of justice and liberation comes.

What Sabbath prohibits is the permanent deployment of power in a community to an elite few. The assumption of such power is a manifestation of idolatry. What Sabbath calls for is the renunciation of the evil powers of this world which corrupt and destroy the creatures of God. These radical requirements were, according to Walter Brueggemann,[5] an effort to bring power relations into a covenantal fabric of neighborliness, for the glorification of individualism is idolatry, and the failure to keep covenant is a sin. Keeping the Sabbath means release from all preoccupations of power: release from the need to produce, release from the need to compete, release from all work and care, in order to devote our undivided attention to our relationship with the God who brings us out of bondage. The Sabbath provides relationship, release, and rest for all. Remember the Sabbath day and keep it holy. Keep the Sabbath and you will remember

---

3. Abraham Joshua Heschel, *The Sabbath* (New York: Farrar, Straus & Young, 1951), 74.

4. Miller, 94.

5. Walter Brueggemann, *The Covenanted Self: Neighborliness and the Limits of Power in God's Realm* (Minneapolis: Fortress Press, 1999), 80.

the redemptive work of God for all God's people. Keep the Sabbath, remember the redemptive work of God, and you will release your neighbor. Keep, remember, release, and you will love your neighbor as yourself. Jesus was a preacher.

Jesus was a preacher, and what did he preach? He preached the restoration of relationship, a restoration begun by looking at the world with different eyes. Empowered by the Spirit, he preached of a world to come and its presence among us now. There's our assignment, preachers. We are to dare to preach of a covenantal relationship between the one, holy God and an entire people who are holy because they are God's own. We are to dare to preach release from the captivity of lesser gods. We are to dare to preach of a realm that is truer than anything we have ever known before. We are to dare to preach that the Scripture is being fulfilled in our hearing. We dare to preach God's kingdom come now. We dare not do otherwise.

Judith M. McDaniel is Howard Chandler Robbins professor of homiletics at Virginia Theological Seminary, Alexandria, Virginia.

Bearing Words of Encouragement

Acts 14:8–18; John 14:23–29
The Feast of St. Barnabas
Linda L. Clader

IT'S HARD for a preacher not to identify with those apostles Jesus is sending out. "Go out there and proclaim the good news, that the reign of God is very close indeed." Travel light. Keep moving. If you're not accepted, just shake the dust off your shoes and move on.

There's a kind of drivenness about it, isn't there? An excitement. An urgency—the urgency that comes with having a message that you just have to pass on.

And there's also the excitement that comes with danger. "I'm sending you out like sheep in the midst of wolves." Preachers, marching out into a hostile world. The apostolic mission—bringing souls to Christ.

Could that be my vocation, too? My big chance! I could really make a mark!

The hair stands up on the back of my neck. My heart races a bit. My breath comes a little quicker, and my hands curl into fists. I recognize the possibility—just the slightest possibility—of becoming a hero.

I wonder whether Barnabas felt anything like that rush of excitement when he got packed off to Antioch. The word had come to the church in Jerusalem: "Some Gentiles up in Antioch have heard the good news and turned to Jesus. So, Barnabas, you'd better get up there to check on things."

There was danger—the danger of the journey itself, of course. And also the danger that perhaps some kind of error was being committed that would cause trouble for the disciples as a whole.

So did Barnabas' heart pound just a little harder than usual as he hurried on his way? His big chance. Antioch was a *big* city, the third biggest city in the Roman Empire. He could really make his mark. He threw on his traveling cloak, and he was off.

Think about what he might have been rolling over in his head as he traveled north. "Have those Gentiles in Antioch been taught the truth? Will there be misinformation I'll have to undo? How do they function together as a community? I'll probably have to clean up their liturgy! I bet they don't know anything about how to run a Sunday school. The Men's Group or the Altar Guild has probably moved into the power vacuum. I'll have to figure out what to do about that."

But when he got there, says Luke, and he "saw the grace of God, he rejoiced and he exhorted them all to remain faithful with steadfast devotion . . . and a great many people were brought to the Lord."

I imagine Barnabas standing at the door of that community in Antioch, still in his traveling garment, looking around. And maybe he *does* see that the liturgy could use a bit of tweaking. And maybe there *is* some work to be done in the area of Christian education.

But that's not what he sees right away. Right away, he sees that the Holy Spirit is already at work in that community. Right away, he sees grace.

Luke tells us that the name, "Barnabas," means "son of encouragement." It's a nickname, because his given name was Joseph. Someone in his community started calling him that for some reason. I'd like to think it was because of this gift he had, the gift of identifying the Spirit's work where it is already happening.

The "Son of Encouragement" identified it, he named the grace, he confirmed its presence, and he gave *that* to the community as a way to help them claim Christ, already in their midst.

In this conference, in this community of *ours*, we talk quite a bit about being bearers of the Word. We recognize the importance of the work we do as preachers. Appropriately, we *exercise* the tools of our trade—we exercise our vocal instruments, we exercise our insights into the Scriptures, we exercise our theological understanding, and we even exercise our spiritual lives, in all their dimensions. We engage in these exercises so we can be better, more effective Word-bearers. Missionaries. Apostles.

But the fact is that most of our apostolic ministry will happen in places and among people who have already encountered Christ. Most of us will make our way to a place that is new to *us*, and discover that it is *not* new to *God*. We will stand in the doorway in our traveling cloaks and look in and see a community where the Spirit is already active, where God's gifts are already being offered and shared—ready to be offered and shared with *us*.

What happens when, instead of focusing on our own responsibility for the proclamation of the Word, we pay attention to recognizing the Word where it has already been spoken? What happens when we tune our ears to the song that is already being sung? What happens when we forget for a while about what we think *we* need to do and concentrate instead on what *God* is already doing, right before our eyes?

What might happen to that vision of ourselves as *hero* that we might secretly enjoy? What might happen to our racing hearts, our shallow breaths, our clenched fists?

A person who isn't panting from running hard is going to be better able to speak God's Word. A person who isn't worrying too much about being effective is more likely to be able to rejoice in the gifts the community is ready to share. A person whose fists aren't clenched with urgency is going to have an easier time raising a hand in blessing or extending it in friendship.

Saint Barnabas, Son of Encouragement, pray for us.

Linda L. Clader is academic dean and professor of homiletics at the Church Divinity School of the Pacific in Berkeley, California. This sermon was delivered at the Preaching Excellence Conference.

Becoming a Martyr

Revelation 7:13–17; Luke 12:2–12
Feast of Bernard Mizeki
Mary Hauck

WHEN I ACCEPTED my first call as vicar in a little pioneer Gothic church in rural California, I discovered that the train went by each and every Sunday during the middle of my sermon. Call me chicken or call me clever, I timed my most controversial statements for 10:23 A.M. on Sunday.

I've since moved on from that little church. In my current parish, the faithful and I assemble week by week to figure out how God wants us to live. I serve God by preaching God's Word, leading worship, helping the vestry cope with an under-financed program for ministry, visiting folks, encouraging lay ministries, and teaching anyone who is curious about Jesus. Most of the time I don't have much use for a train. Most days are ordinary days. A few days are special.

Today we observe Bernard Mizeki's special day. Bernard was a lay catechist who came with his bishop in 1891 from Mozambique to an area of Africa that is now Zimbabwe. His actual day is June 18, but I don't think he would have considered June 18 his special day. I don't think he even wanted to be on the church calendar at all. Bernard was having a fine time praying the Anglican hours each day, tending his subsistence garden, studying the local language, making friends with the villagers, and teaching their little children about Jesus.

He had no idea that June 18, 1896, would eventually become his special day on the church calendar, marked out in red for martyrs. Now in the sense that martyr means "bear witness to," Bernard was all about being faithful to that call. When Bernard Mizeki was warned to leave during an uprising between African nationalists and missionaries, he simply stayed put. He rejected the idea that he was working for the European colonial governments. He said he was working for Christ. And he chose to remain faithful to his community.

On June 18, 1896, Bernard was murdered outside his hut—impaled by a spear. The church has since named June 18 a holy day, Bernard Mizeki's special day, the day we commemorate him as a catechist and a martyr— "martyr" in the sense that means "a witness unto death."

"Almighty God, who kindled the flame of your love in the heart of your holy martyr Bernard Mizeki," we pray. This is when I wish a train would go by, because if you asked Bernard if he'd rather be a holy martyr or a lay catechist, I bet he'd choose catechist. Just like if you asked Oscar Romero if he'd rather be a martyr or keep passing out the blessed Body of Christ in El Salvador, he'd opt for a long, rich life of ministry among God's beloved, instead of being murdered in the middle of the Eucharist.

Did they choose to be faithful in the face of personal danger? Yes. Does the fact that they died while being faithful to Christ make them a martyr? Well, again, yes. But mostly what they were doing was being faithful. Life found them in the act of being faithful. Death found them in the act of being faithful. John Claypool described a witness as "a truth bearer of their own experience."[1] These two were bearing witness even unto death.

---

1. John Claypool, in his lecture at the *Preaching Excellence Program*, at Villanova University, June 5, 2002.

As a young child growing up in an Anglo-Catholic household, I had a morbid fascination with Fox's *Lives of the Saints*, which sat on my parents' bookshelves between *The Language of Flowers* and *Expectant Motherhood*. The *Lives of the Saints* fascinated me because I loved the Lord Jesus, too. And I wondered if I could be noble enough to die for him—to be a martyr.

The Anchor Bible Dictionary has this to say about martyrs:

Simply put martyrdom refers to the act of choosing death rather than renouncing one's religious principles. Death then is voluntary, but not wholly so, since some element of compulsion exists, and some noble cause is at stake.[2]

"Who are these," John's Revelation asks, "robed in white, and where have they come from?" "These are they who have come out of the great ordeal; they have washed their robes and made them white in the blood of the lamb." When I heard it as a child, this passage from Revelation seemed like a page out of Fox's *Lives*—distant—meant to describe times long ago and far away. In my preaching life, this text pops up regularly at burial services for dead Christians and on holy days for long-dead martyrs. It describes a vision of heaven, meant to comfort and reassure.

But that was before the world got so small. Before Oscar Romero and Bernard Mizeki and China and Tibet and synagogue burnings in California and jumbo jets flying into buildings in the name of God.

What are we to make of the concept of martyrdom now? And what are we to say about it as preachers? Is there a difference between taking one's life directly and allowing one's life to be taken? What about when other people (who don't want it to be their special day) get taken with you? What about Jesus as a martyr? It is clear in all the Gospels that his death was voluntary. "No one takes my life from me, but I lay it down of my own accord," Jesus asserts in the Gospel according to John.

The early Church took the model of Jesus as faithful martyr seriously. By the second and third centuries, the church calendar had become packed and the rush to Christian martyrdom had become . . . well, a problem. We are more cautious now. *The Anchor Bible Dictionary* says:

"It is seldom clear under what circumstances one is to offer up one's life, whether one can take a hand in one's own execution, and whether one should avail oneself of the opportunity for escape."[3]

---

2. *The Anchor Bible Dictionary* (New York: Doubleday, 1992), IV, 574.
3. Ibid., 578.

For most of us, and for most of the folks we'll preach to, martyrdom as a reality is a new blip on the radar screen. It's not confined to dusty books anymore. And it's unclear how much more real it's going to get. It's unclear.

What *is* clear? That we are called to a life of faithfulness. Part of that life is honest and faithful preaching. The Gospel of Jesus Christ asserts that *this* is clear: "Nothing is covered up that will not be uncovered, and nothing secret that will not become known . . . what you have whispered behind closed doors will be proclaimed from the housetops!" The Gospel has been unleashed in this world. It won't be silent.

The Gospel says *this* is clear: "Everyone who acknowledges me before others, the Son of Man also will acknowledge before the angels of God."

Preachers are to be truth-bearing witnesses to the Gospel of Jesus Christ even if it makes them uncomfortable and they wish a train would go by to drown out their words. God is faithful. God gives a promise. When we answer this call, when we prayerfully and honestly trust God in this endeavor to live and preach faithfully, God promises: "When they bring you before the synagogues, the rulers, and the authorities, do not worry about how you are to defend yourselves or what you are to say; for the Holy Spirit will teach you at that very hour what you ought to say."

Mary Hauck is rector of St. Clement's Church in Rancho Cordova, California. This sermon was delivered at the Preaching Excellence Conference.

UPLIFTING ELEMENTS IN PROPHETIC LEADERSHIP

Enfleshing the Word

Job 29:7–11; Acts 9:1–20
William J. Eakins

When I went out to the gate of the city, When I took my seat in the square,
The young men saw me and withdrew, And the aged rose up and stood;
The nobles refrained from talking And laid their hands on their mouths.
When the ear heard, it commended me, And when the eye saw, it approved.

JOB'S REVERIE about his past acclaim echoes the secret dream of many a would-be preacher. The Preaching Conference version might go like this: When I rose up to deliver my sermon, the preaching group fell into a rapt silence. When I began to speak, all beamed with holy wonder and the faculty exclaimed in hushed tones, "Who is this golden-tongued spellbinder, this latter-day Chrysostom who stands before us?" The rector's version of the preacher's dream is similar: When I climbed into the pulpit, the children looked up expectantly, their elders nodded sage agreement, and the vestry smiled contentedly to each other as if to say, "How blessed is St. Swithin's to have such a fine priest as this!"

Sounds pretty good, doesn't it? Who among us would not enjoy an approval rating like that? The trouble, however, comes when we preachers mistake the winning of such approval as our ministry.

A wise old priest who befriended me when I was newly ordained knew better. I still have the book he gave me with his inscription on the flyleaf, "Your ministry is to draw aside the curtain and reveal Christ. But always," he added, "be sure to hide yourself in the folds."

Preaching is an act of revelation, of making known that which has been hidden, an act in which the preacher is privileged to play a central part. However, the crucial point is that the one we are to reveal is not ourselves but Jesus Christ.

Can we see a model for our ministry as preachers in the experience of the apostle Paul that we heard about in Acts? Paul, full of himself and his preconceived ideas of who God is and what God is about, bustles up to Damascus to continue his persecution of the followers of Christ. But on the dusty road outside the city gates, Paul is driven to his knees by a shining vision, one that illumines him and at the same time blinds him.

In a flash of divine revelation Paul sees that Jesus really is God's anointed one, the longed-for Christ. But, ironically, Paul's burst of spiritual insight is accompanied by physical blindness. Perhaps the blindness was intended to teach proud, self-reliant Paul how much he would need to rely upon God from then on. Perhaps the blindness was meant to teach Paul how thoroughly life-changing is the Gospel that had now been revealed to him.

Whatever the reason for the blindness may be, the reason Paul regains his sight is clear. "Brother," says Ananias, "the Lord Jesus . . . has sent me so that you may regain your sight and be filled with the Holy Spirit." "And immediately," we are told, "something like scales fell from [Paul's] eyes, and his sight was restored."

What is the result of this eye-opening experience? "Immediately he began to proclaim Jesus . . . saying, 'He is the Son of God.'" Paul receives his sight and goes to enable others to see as well. "I once was lost but now am found, was blind but now I see." The line from John Newton's familiar hymn sings the apostle's conversion. And so Paul sets out to fulfill his great missionary work of carrying the light of Christ out into the dark night of a waiting world.

The world is still full of much darkness and the world is still waiting for the light of Christ to bring clear vision and life-changing love. People are yearning to hear Good News about who God is, how God loves this world, even a world where young Palestinians strap bombs to themselves, where kids shoot other kids in school, where some countries worry about obesity while others face starvation.

People long to hear how God could love such a mixed-up, violent, unjust world such as this, love it so much that God became one of us in Jesus, how God kept on loving us even when we nailed Jesus to a cross and kept on loving us so much that God raised Jesus from the dead. People are yearning to hear Good News about how God keeps on loving the world right now, loving it so much that God's powerful spirit is at work to heal and renew the whole earth and each and every one of us.

People are looking for Good News that will give them light and sight to journey on. And it is the privilege and the responsibility of every preacher so to proclaim the Good News about Jesus Christ that the groping blind will see and rejoice.

Like Paul, however, we preachers must first see ourselves if we are to help others gain their sight. St. Francis put it another way: "The preacher must first grow hot within before speaking words which in themselves are cold." Phillip Brooks said it like this: "Preaching is truth mediated through personality." In other words, the preacher is not the message, but the preacher is the vital medium through which the message is delivered and received.

Preaching is thus inescapably personal. Just as the Word was made flesh in Jesus, so the Word must become flesh and dwell in us. We must wrestle with Holy Scripture and claim its truth and its promises for our own lives. We must hear the Good News of God's love until we not only know that God so loves the world but that God loves even you . . . and me. You and I must discover what it means for each of us to call Jesus Savior and Lord. Then we need to tell our stories in ways that others can hear. And if we are human and if we are honest, they will.

A nineteenth-century missionary in the South Pacific arrived at his home base after a long week of preaching the Gospel on a number of small neighboring islands when a messenger arrived with an invitation to come over to another island and speak there. The preacher was exhausted, maybe like us here at this preaching conference, and wanted to stay home. He summoned his native assistant and gave him an evangelistic tract, telling the man to go in his place and read the message to the islanders. But the assistant knew better. "No, Father, the people on that island don't want me to read to them; they want to read you." The Gospel is not just words. It is the Word made flesh in the preacher.

Reflect for a moment on what you know about the Crimean War. When did it happen? Why did it happen? Who was fighting whom? Most of us are pretty vague about the facts. True, some may recall the Charge of the Light Brigade, but who remembers who was charging whom? But what just about all of us remember clearly about the Crimean War is a woman and her love. Florence Nightingale—we hear her name and we can picture the heroic lady with a lamp, making her night rounds of the sick and dying, bringing light and love to those who lay in darkness. Disembodied propositions and abstract data quickly fade into nothingness. God's love, God's truth incarnate in human personality is what endures.

Like Paul and Barnabas and a multitude of other Christian witnesses before us, we preachers of today have the responsibility and privilege of bearing the Light of Christ to a waiting world. Our task is to let the Word of God dwell in us richly. Our hearers may never be moved by our logic or by our eloquence; they may never remember a single word we've said let alone remember the outlines of our sermons. But if we burn with the Light of those who know the living God, then they will remember us with gratitude and, more importantly, they will remember the One we have revealed.

William J. Eakins is retired rector of Trinity Church, Hartford, Connecticut. This sermon was delivered at the Preaching Excellence Conference.

Let Your Words Be Few . . . And Powerful

Ecclesiastes 5:1–20
Hope H. Eakins

IS YOUR sermon ready? Are its crisp pages in a manila folder in your briefcase, numbered sequentially, free of scribbles? Have you preached it to your spouse, your roommate, your cat? Have you stood before a mirror and practiced your gestures? Or could it be that you are still a little anxious about it?

Even at this moment, I am. You know, the faculty at this conference are not immune to the desire to preach like St. John Chrysostom. We want to do that for the glory of God of course, but, if the truth were told, one or two of us might also have an occasional desire—just a small one, mind you—for some personal glory as well. And if that is so, the words of Ecclesiastes in the first lesson should challenge us all, "Never be rash with your mouth . . . let your words be few, for the fool's voice comes with many words."

It makes you stop and think, doesn't it, as we gather here for a week of words, a week during which each of us will hear at least thirty-six sermons? "Never be rash with your mouth . . . let your words be few, for the fool's voice comes with many words." Now the author of Ecclesiastes identifies himself by the name Qoheleth, which presumably means something like "gatherer of proverbs," but for many generations the word has been translated as "preacher," and not just *a* preacher, but *the* Preacher, so it seems that we would do well to regard his counsel as we open this conference for preachers. The way Qoheleth begins the book is this: "Vanity of vanities, says the Preacher," and then he instructs us not to be too quick to utter a word before God. So it seems kind of daunting to be up here; it seems like a body might just bow her head reverently and then go sit down.

Qoheleth is right. Preaching is not a responsibility to be taken lightly. Writing sermons is hard work. It doesn't matter if you were an English major for four years or if you worked as a journalist for ten years or lectured as a professor for twenty. It doesn't matter how long you have been preaching. It doesn't matter if you are speaking to a congregation that loves you or speaking to faces you have never seen before—preaching is hard work.

It has never been easy for preachers. John, called Chrysostom, was dubbed John the Golden Tongue for his homiletic eloquence. His style was said to be elaborate, sinewy, and incisive, and, according to the *Encyclopedia Britannica,* he often had to chide people for applauding during his sermons. Now John's fine words may have come flowing from his mouth, but I imagine that they did not flow as easily from his pen, that like the rest of us, John had to labor long and hard to craft those words before he set foot in a pulpit.

Preaching is an endeavor that requires pain and courage and humility, and if it doesn't demand those things, then it is not really preaching. Preaching is painful because the preacher's heart is the place where the word of God and the words of God's people get all mixed up together, and that means that the preacher's heart has to stretch until it nearly breaks trying to hold both the pathos of it all and the joy of it all.

It was hard for preachers on September 11, when the world cried out to hear God's word, when those given into our care wanted comfort and understanding, or worse yet, wanted retribution and vengeance. And those of us who had the temerity to step into pulpits that day needed comfort and understanding ourselves, for our throats ached with the crying and our hearts were sore with the raw need to make sense of it all. But we had no time, had no choice but to stand there and speak as much to our own need as to the needs of the world. We found the courage to speak that day and in the weeks that followed because, whether we were ordained or not, we were all under God's holy orders to remember the old, old story and to proclaim that, no matter how bleak the wilderness, God will send manna to nourish us and a pillar of light to lead us on our way.

It will be hard for me to get into the pulpit next Sunday when I go back to my parish to preach to a congregation that is asking the same question they asked on September 11: Why, Lord? Why? For you see, some months ago the beautiful young bride who was to be married there this week ordered the flowers for her wedding, white hydrangeas and fragrant lilies and sweet peas to fill the church. And the flowers will be there. But the bride and groom won't be there for the wedding, because Kathleen was struck by a train and killed before she could walk down the aisle.

And it is not just tragedy that challenges the preacher. It is joy as well. How can our poor words ever name and illumine the Love that drew this couple together in the first place? How can we describe the joy of a birth to a barren wife, the generosity of a community that gathers its riches to give them away? Paul says, "No eye has seen, nor ear heard, nor heart conceived what God has prepared for those who love God." And we preachers have the audacity to try to name it and describe it all.

Qoheleth the Preacher is right. We should not be rash with our mouths. Jesus got a little more specific about that. He warned us that what comes out of our mouths can defile us in ways that are far worse than bad sermons—fornication, theft, false witness, and slander, to name a few of them. It's a wonder anyone is ever brave enough to step into a pulpit. "Guard your steps when you go to the house of God," says Qoheleth the Preacher; and we should, we should guard them.

Qoheleth calls us to guard against falsehood and faithlessness, to live lives of integrity, to pay our vows to the Lord, because if we don't, we are no more than debaters assigned to argue one side of a question, no matter whether they believe it or not.

We have a hard task, measuring the truth of our lives against the truth of God's word. And it is hard because in order to preach hope, we have to be people who see hope and declare God's promises in the midst of pain, people who can dream of a Kingdom that just might dawn on earth as it is in heaven. It is hard, because in order to preach love, we have to be lovers, people who take the risk of loving, people who know the ineffable joy of being one with our beloved. It is hard, because to preach about stewardship we have to be generous givers, people who have poured themselves out when there was not enough to go around, and, in the pouring, discovered that God fills our hands only when they are empty.

Qoheleth was not what you would call a religious man, but he knew the value of integrity. "God has no pleasure in fools," he wrote. Nor do our congregations. What's more, they can smell a fool a mile away.

Qoheleth is a preacher for the worst of times. He is a preacher for today. Qoheleth sees the injustice and hopelessness in life; he knows that the poor are always with us. He knows that all the money in the world will never make us happy; as a matter of fact, he says that if we are rich, we will have sleepless nights worrying about it. The worst sin for Qoheleth is not idolatry or injustice or greed. The worst sin is failing to appreciate God's good gifts. His admonition to 'eat-drink-and-be-merry' is not a selfish hedonism but a godly commandment. All is vanity, says the Preacher; God is inscrutable and our work achieves nothing. But what we do know is that we are created to enjoy God's blessings, and we are fools if we pass them by. All may be vanity, all a fleeting breath, but life is worth living. Jesus said it a better way: "I came that they might have life and have it abundantly."

And so the task for us preachers is to proclaim God's grace and abundance, to declare that life is more than a time to be born and a time to die, because God made this world for us to relish it, to taste and see that the Lord is good, and to discover the blessings of a grateful heart. God made this world for us, when God spoke a word into the primordial chaos to separate the light from the darkness, the sea from the dry land, to bring order out of chaos.

God *said*, "Let there be light," and God's strong Word cleaved the darkness and then God set us smack in the middle of it all and invited us, commanded us actually, to do the same thing. And here is where things get scary, for when preachers speak the word of the Lord, their words have power, power to bring order from chaos, power to shape and heal the world, power to bring unity in the face of division, to make peace in the face of war, and to render justice for the oppressed.

The story is told of a keynote speaker at a preaching conference who strode up to the pulpit with a sheaf of papers in his hand. Trying to describe the great responsibility of preaching, he held up his thick manuscript and asked rhetorically, "Where to begin? Where to begin?" And a voice came from the audience, "As close to the end as possible."

That is very good advice, and it is also the counsel of Qoheleth the Preacher who tells us to make every word count. I don't think he was promoting cute little homilettes, or even well-crafted one-point sermons, but I think Qoheleth would agree that you should get to the heart of the matter and start as close to the end as possible.

What do you say in the face of tragedy? What do you say when the poor are oppressed and justice is violated in the land? You say that God loved us enough to make a world, and that God will keep on loving us no matter what. You start as close to the end as possible; you start with the Good News that there is no sin too bad to be forgiven, no child too small to count, no injustice too great to be vanquished.

And the wonderful thing is that once we get inspired, once God's Spirit breathes into us with that Word that is sharper than a two-edged sword, that Word then has the power to renew not only the world, but to renew *us*.

Hope H. Eakins is retired rector of St. John's Church, Essex, Connecticut. This sermon was delivered at the Preaching Excellence Conference.

AFFIRMING THE CORPORATE NATURE OF PROPHETIC WITNESS

You Is Plural!

Luke 17:5–10
Proper 22 C
Michael S. White

AS A SOUTHERNER, I have my share of language usage that is not "proper" by academic standards; but there is one particular language use with which I have a hard time. I cannot grasp the fact that *you* can be plural. For me, the word you is singular, and *ya'll* is plural; or, minimally, *you all* is plural. If you say, "How are you doing?" I assume that you are speaking to one person. If you say "How are ya'll doing," I assume that you are talking to a group. Southerners are not alone in this struggle. Some other regions of the country solve this problem with "you guys" or even "yous guys."

It would have been easier if the rules of proper English provided a different word for *you* (plural) from the word *you* (singular). Our liturgy uses *you* as plural. When I say, "The Lord be with you," this is a plural *you*. I have threatened to surprise everyone and one day say, "The Lord be with ya'll."

With my trouble with *you* and *ya'll* in mind, listen to the words of our Gospel lesson. The Lord replied, "If you had faith the size of a mustard seed, you could say to this mulberry tree, 'Be uprooted and planted in the sea,' and it would obey you."

To be honest, this seems more than a little out of the reach of my faith. While at Wrightsville Beach or in Boone, I never once tried to see if I had the faith of a mustard seed. If I do have even the smallest bit of faith, then I should be able to say to the tree at the beach "Be planted in the sea," or to the mountains around Boone, "Be thrown all the way over to the coast," and expect that it will happen.

But, before we completely dismiss that as out of reach, let's look at this text more closely.

"The *apostles* said to the Lord, 'Increase *our* faith!'" It is not "Peter said to the Lord" or "James or John said to the Lord," but "*The apostles*"—plural—"said to the Lord, 'Increase *our* faith!'" And, the Lord replied, "If *you* had faith the size of a mustard seed, *you* could say to this mulberry tree, 'Be uprooted and planted in the sea' and it would obey *you.*"

This passage is not saying that any *one* of us can move a mountain or uproot a tree, but that all of us together can do anything we set our minds and hearts to do. I told the assistant rector about my hunch that the *you* in this passage (that has so often been individualized and applied to a personal faith) is actually a *plural you.* After all, the question comes from a group and is answered to a group of believers. Joshua offered to use one of his books to check the Greek *you* in this passage. I said, "Sure, but I really like this line of thought, so if it is a singular *you,* maybe you shouldn't tell me." A few minutes later, Joshua returned with a smile and said, "All of these usages of *you* are plural."

So, the proper reading of this passage tells us that I can't move a mountain. You can't uproot a tree and send it into the sea. But, we can—you all can—ya'll can—yous guys can. *You* is plural.

If you want an image of moving a mountain or a tree, just picture the firefighters and rescue workers removing the rubble of the twin towers a bucket at a time. They pass a bucket of ash and dust from hand to hand to hand. They have already made great progress in moving this mountain, this tree. Rather than picture a tree or mountain leaping through the air, picture all of us with shovels and buckets.

No, I can't move a mountain, and you can't move a tree, but we can. And, this principle of faith applies to all areas of life. We can! This teaching of Jesus says that we really do need each other.

My family and I, my household, cannot move a mountain. But, joining in unity with many families, many households, it begins to seem possible. It would be really pushing us for St. Luke's to build an entire Habitat house alone, but we are presently building a house with the Episcopal and Lutheran congregations of Durham. Together, we can build a house one nail at a time.

If we desire to have peace in our community, we have to reach across the lines that divide us: racial, religious, economic, and political. We must reach out to all types and kinds of people. If our nation is going to try to uproot the tree of terrorism, it cannot be just the singular nation, it has to be we, the many nations.

We are all connected. The world is shrinking. What happens in one place really does affect the rest of the world now. If we truly desire peace in our world, we as a nation are being forced to reach across seas to nations that are culturally and ideologically very different from us.

When we think as *we* instead of just *me*, we can do anything we set our hearts and minds to do. Remember, and help me to remember, that *you* is plural. It takes all of us. If all of us simply have faith the size of a tiny mustard seed, then together God can use us to do things that are beyond our ability to ask or believe. God can use "us" to move and build mountains and to plant trees.

"The apostles said to the Lord, 'Increase our faith!'" We say, "Lord, increase our faith!" And, the Lord replies to us, "If ya'll had faith the size of a mustard seed, ya'll could say to this mulberry tree, 'Be uprooted and planted in the sea' and it would obey ya'll."

Michael S. White is rector of St. Luke's Church,
Durham, North Carolina.

Harvest Evangelism

Matthew 9:35–10:8
Proper 6 A
Thomas Mustard

DAUGHTER MOLLY gave me a collection of Charles Schultz's "Peanuts" comic strips for my last birthday. In one of them Linus is listening attentively as Lucy tells him about her potential as an evangelist. She says to Linus, "I would have made a good evangelist. Do you know that kid who sits behind me at school? I convinced him that my religion is better than his religion." "How did you do that?" Linus asks. Lucy replies, "I hit him over the head with my lunch box."

Somehow I don't believe that is what Jesus had in mind when he said, "The harvest is plentiful, but the laborers are few." But evidence confirms that many religious people, Christian and otherwise, seem to think that hitting people over the head with lunch boxes, or weapons designed to do more than put knots on the head, is an acceptable method of evangelism.

In the summer and early fall on the farm where I grew up, we would have a number of harvest times. We would bale hay regularly throughout the summer, and that chore was routine. But, when the oats, wheat, and corn were ready for harvest, an air of urgency became detectable. When those harvest times came, life took on a no-nonsense character.

Harvest times were cooperative efforts. Usually, a couple of other farmers would bring various pieces of equipment and any strong males who were available. My grandmother, mother, and aunts would pool their efforts to feed such a large crew. Days started early and often ended late. There was a kind of unspoken understanding that the success of the harvest depended on the collective efforts of everyone. The work of each was related to that of another. Equipment and tools had been properly serviced; necessary supplies like gas, oil, and grease were readily available. Toolboxes were stocked with every size wrench, screwdriver, and pliers. All kinds of nuts and bolts were inside the boxes, ready for any needed repairs.

Harvest times were somehow different from regular times. During normal times, we young folk would be allowed occasionally to take a dip in our homemade swimming hole. Sometimes we would even take a bar of soap and wash. But harvest times were different. We knew not to ask if we could go swimming or play baseball. I would envy my friends in town who got to go to the Lions' Club pool or over to Hungry Mother State Park.

Sometimes during normal times we would come across a small snake and start to play with it or find a nest of baby rabbits and chase them across the field. But we knew that during harvest times no such frivolity would be tolerated. Granddaddy A. T. monitored our activities and handed out passing or failing grades. The work ethic was always reinforced with the words, "Now, Tommy, don't be shiftless!"

I have thought about harvest times on the farm from time to time. I got to thinking about that again this past week after reading the Gospel for this Sunday. Jesus said, "The harvest is plentiful, but the laborers are few." Jesus was looking at a vast collection of human beings, those who were harassed and helpless, like sheep without a shepherd. He wasn't thinking about a wheat field, but the analogy would apply and the disciples understood it perfectly. Harvest time had arrived. The crop was ready and workers were needed.

So, Jesus gives harvest instructions to the twelve, to those who would become his disciples. Notice the air of urgency, the no-nonsense approach in Jesus' instructions. Don't get distracted; keep the primary task in view.

There are certain things about these instructions and the harvest times from the days of my youth that may apply to the way we live as Christians.

First, look at the mutual trust. There was a mission to be performed. All needed for a successful harvest had been provided. Rain and sunshine had come; proper fertilizing, hoeing, spraying, and weeding had been faithfully done. Then came the time for trust. Trust that the crop had reached maturity, that the harvest was not too early, that the maximum yield could be expected. Trust that those who had been a part of hundreds of harvests knew the crop and could tell by various signs when the time was right. Trust that the tools and equipment had been properly maintained and were in good working order.

Jesus sends his disciples into the harvest with that element of trust. Everything necessary for a successful harvest has been provided. There needs to be an element of trust in the message and in the fact that God will prepare the field, if we will just show up ready to go to work. Not much will happen if we are guilty of spiritual shiftlessness.

Second, look at the element of interdependence. Harvest time, as I experienced it, was not the time to rank what one was doing over against the work of another. Every job was important, and all the jobs related to and built on one another. If one job was not being done, everyone suffered. If the water boy/girl didn't keep a fresh supply of cool spring water on hand, Old Fred would start to yell and would stop his tractor and yell some more, until delivery was made.

Notice that this element of interdependence is found in the listing of the disciples whom Jesus sent out first into the harvest. They are listed in pairs. They are sent out in twos. They need mutual sharing and support. Jesus knows far better than most that the isolated, self-contained Christian will be heir to all sorts of misunderstandings and prone to head off down the wrong path. Our bishop is correct when he says, "There is no such thing as a Christian alone; there is no such things as a congregation alone." At least going out two-by-two gives a much better chance of being good laborers. Good evangelism always has an element of interdependence to it.

Third, there is an element of glorification. Harvests would often end after dark. Bone-weary laborers would flop down in chairs and on beds without saying much to anyone. But there was deep satisfaction felt in the muscles as well as the heart. There was a kind of glorification felt in having been faithful to God, to the created order, to the harvest. There was no whooping and hollering, no slaps on the back, no high-fives, no audience to applaud, no congregation to comment on the quality, or lack thereof, of the work. There was just the internal satisfaction that comes from being faithful, doing what was expected.

It has been my experience that working in the "people harvest," when it is done the way Jesus instructed, is much the same. No name up in lights and no notice of a job well done in the *Bedford Bulletin*, just a feeling that somehow God has been glorified by what we have done. Harvest time reminds us that God does not call us to be successful, just faithful.

People might not notice. It's okay that they don't. God notices. God says, "Well done, good and faithful servant." And that's enough!

So, dear people of God, harvest time has come. And we will be faithful laborers if we remember that God can always be trusted, remember that we work best when we realize how much we need each other, and remember whom it is that we are to glorify.

If we will do that, we won't have to hit others over the head and call it evangelism.

Thomas Mustard is rector of St. John's Church, Bedford, Virginia.

From That Time

1 Corinthians 1:10–17; Matthew 4:12–23
Epiphany 3 A
Malcolm C. Young

WHEN THE Civil War broke out, Mark Twain had to make a decision. His mother supported the Confederacy. His brother had campaigned for Lincoln. Although he flirted with joining a local regiment, ultimately he went west to the new territory of Nevada. "Without having been trained," he said, "I knew more about retreating than the man who had invented retreating."[1]

This week Jesus retreats. "When Jesus heard that John had been arrested," Matthew tells us, "he withdrew to Galilee. He left Nazareth and made his home in Capernaum." The Bible often mentions how important it was for Jesus to get away from the crowds so that he could pray in solitude to his Father. But this is different. When Herod imprisons Jesus' cousin at an isolated fortress east of the Dead Sea, Jesus heads still further north.

Is Jesus afraid? I think he probably is. Is Jesus a coward? Is he simply trying to protect himself? I don't think so. We cannot be certain of Jesus' motivations. All we know is that when Herod captures John, everything changes for Jesus. At this terrible moment Jesus alters his approach to ministry completely.

---

1. Theconnection.org for 14 January 2002 (11'00").

We do not know much about Jesus' ministry before this time. It started after his baptism and his temptation by Satan in the wilderness. Initially it appears that Jesus worked mostly alone. It seems as if this was a ministry directed primarily toward the people he would have regarded as most like himself, the people in his own home town. We do not know the content of his message, but people there did not seem to hear him. Later he says, "Prophets are not without honor except in their own country and in their own house." Matthew also explains that Jesus "did not do many deeds of power there because of their unbelief."

When he hears about John's suffering, Jesus is transformed. He does not go into hiding. He does not maintain a low profile at home among the people most likely to protect him. Instead Jesus radically changes his strategy. This morning I am going to consider two revolutionary changes in Jesus' ministry after this tragedy and their importance to us.

"When Jesus heard that John had been arrested . . . he left Nazareth and made his home in . . . Galilee of the Gentiles."[2] The first thing Jesus does when he wants to change his ministry is to leave home. He leaves his friends, his relatives, the people who share his customs and religion. He goes to Galilee of the Gentiles, to strangers who do not understand his faith.

When I was in high school I wanted to become a minister because I believed that the Christian life is beautiful and true. I knew many people who seemed lost, people who had not yet found Christ and as a result did not know either God or themselves. I became a priest because of them. The strangest thing is that all these years later, the more I work for the church, the less I have anything to do with this group of people.

Only twenty-seven percent of the people on the Peninsula attend weekly religious services. This compares with forty-one percent nationwide.[3] Right now most of my energies go into only a tiny fraction of those who go to church. The people who come to this place, the center of my life on weekdays and weekends, the people I work with and care for and socialize with are almost all Christians. I feel at home with them. We share a set of similar aims and values, a language for talking about what makes our life meaningful.

But Jesus left home. This week I have been asking myself what it would mean for us as a church to leave home. What would it mean for us at

---

2. This is a little strange. According to the map Nazareth is in Galilee but near its southern border. Maybe Matthew means that part of Galilee where the Gentiles are.

3. Study by the Peninsula Community Foundation cited in *Transfiguration's* January 2002 newsletter. This study also found that people in other communities are ten percent more likely to socialize with co-workers off the job and as a whole socialize twenty-two percent more than do we.

Christ Church if we focused more on proclaiming the Gospel to people who had not heard it and less on sustaining the faith of people who are already in the know?

I have to confess that this is both a frightening and an exciting question for me. It makes me anxious because I know that what we do now nourishes me deeply. When it comes to how we pray I may be the most conservative person here. And this is the reason. Some of the words and expressions we use as part of our worship today go back almost two thousand years. When we say, "Lift up your hearts," we are repeating the same words Jesus heard as a boy at Passover. We say, "The Lord be with you," in exactly the same way that first-century Christian martyrs did.[4] I love this connection to the saints who came before us. Their experiences of God and hopes for the future are still with us as we worship. That we might lose some of this frightens me.

Still the idea of Christ Church leaving home is also exciting, because Christianity was never intended to be only for the people who have already heard the good news. Its outward expressions have always been in the process of changing in order to include newcomers.

When you leave home and begin to meet strangers, you will always have questions about your identity. To be a church for people in Santa Clara County who have not heard the good news, we will certainly have to change. The crucial question is: How much can we change to welcome new members of the body of Christ and yet still maintain our identity as Christians who value a particular tradition?

The second change that Jesus makes after hearing the news about John is that he stops working alone. After his baptism, Jesus knows that *he* will never be the same. After Jesus starts to ask others for their help, the *world* will never be the same.

All the churches and cathedrals in the world, all the Christian books and theologies, the charitable institutions, but most importantly all the lives that have been changed—all this started when Jesus first asked for help. Your ministry also will be much stronger when you ask for help. Our ministry together in this church will be far more powerful when we work together and when we invite others to join us. But don't think that it will be easier.

A young rabbi felt exasperated by a serious problem in his congregation. Every week during Friday services, half the congregation stood for prayers and half remained seated. Each group shouted at the other, argu-

---

4. Marion J. Hatchett, *Commentary on the American Prayer Book* (New York: Seabury Press, 1981), 290–92.

ing that they were the ones upholding tradition. Nothing that the young rabbi did seemed to help. Fortunately, he discovered that the ninety-nine-year-old founder of the synagogue lived nearby at a retirement home in northern Marin County. The young rabbi went and asked him, "Was it the tradition in the beginning to stand during prayers?" The old rabbi said, "No." "Oh, so it was the tradition to sit," responded the young rabbi. "No," answered the old man. This exasperated the young rabbi. "What we have now is complete chaos. Some people stand, the others sit and everyone is always yelling at each other." "Ah," said the old man, "*that* was the tradition."[5]

That is our tradition too, from the beginning. Paul wrote letters to the first churches that are filled with embarrassing pleading that they should become "one body in Christ." (Those letters represent something like one fourth of the New Testament.) He pleads, "I appeal to you that there be no more divisions among you." People of true faith have always disagreed.

But this does not seem to bother Jesus at all. He simply says, "Follow me!" These disciples were difficult to teach. Their actions made it seem like they didn't understand who he was. They argued about which of them was the greatest. They broke Jesus' heart by betraying him before the Roman army could break his body. But Jesus still says, "Follow me!"

First there were two, then four, then twelve. Today the body of Christ includes billions of people who believe in God's power to overcome hatred, billions of people who believe in love.

Perhaps the most valuable advice I ever received from an older priest was this: There always exists a trade-off between efficiency and participation. If you want things to work well, do not involve many people. If you want things to work perfectly, then do it yourself. This old man told me that in church life you cannot escape the trade-off between efficiency and participation. But, he added, always err on the side of participation.

When Jesus is threatened by terrible tragedy, he changes the way he does ministry and in doing so he changes the world. Jesus does two simple things that transform his ministry. He leaves home and he asks for help.

Brothers and sisters, Jesus is with us this morning. He looks at us with great love in his eyes because he knows how we are suffering. Jesus also knows that leaving home and asking for help are difficult. But still he says, "Follow me!"

Malcolm C. Young is rector of Christ Church, Los Altos, California.

---

5. From Barbara Lemmel, "Makeshift Communities," in *Christian Century* January 6–13, 1999.

PROVIDING FRESH REMINDERS
OF UNCOMFORTABLE TRUTHS

Infection of Mercy

Matthew 9:9–13
Proper 5 A
J. Michael Ehmer

ONE DAY God looked down upon Earth, noticed all of the mischievous behavior going on, and decided to send an angel to check it out. When the angel returned, the report was not good: Ninety-five percent of the people on earth were misbehaving; only five percent were not. God decided to send an e-mail to all the members of the good group—the five percent—to give them some encouragement. And do you know what that e-mail said? . . . Oh, I see that none of you got a copy either!

We're always lumping people into categories, aren't we? Good and bad, right and wrong, those who are like us and those who are not. We have an instinct for building walls—walls that either keep others out or keep us in.

When we think of walls, many of us immediately envision prisons. They certainly have walls—walls that are designed to keep the inmates *in,* to separate them from the rest of society, to punish "them" and protect "us." But most of society's walls have the opposite purpose: to keep others *out.* Perhaps the best known of these are associated with national security assets, like military bases.

When I flew B-52s in the Air Force, we were still pulling around-the-clock ground alert. We had to stay close to the parked aircraft that were loaded with bombs and ready for immediate take off. We lived in what was called an "alert facility." It had double, twenty-foot-high fences with razor wire all around. Armed guards in towers and roving patrols observed the entire area. Gaining entry involved extensive searches. All this was not to keep undesirable people in but to keep them out.

In ancient times, cities did a similar thing. Communities built walls for security—to keep the bad guys out. When Sue-Ann and I lived in Germany, we used to love to go to the old, walled-city of Rottenburg. It was easy to see how the walls would have offered protection from their enemies and why, when there was danger, the people from the rural areas all flocked into the safety of the city.

But there was another side to this situation as well. During the Middle Ages, when the Black Death was sweeping across Europe, the areas most severely affected were the walled cities. The plague seemed to thrive within the high concentration of people and animals. These confined cities made the perfect breeding ground for the rats and fleas that carried the illness. Ironically, it was their safe, protected environment that led to their demise. If they had been spread out in the countryside, they would have had a much better chance of avoiding the disease.

There aren't many walled cities today. Technology makes them useless. Even the Berlin Wall has come down. But there are other forms of walls that remain. Although medical science has made dramatic advances against communicable diseases, there are still some situations where it's best to isolate people from others. Sometimes being around other people endangers individuals; for example, when their immune systems are very weak, being around others can endanger some individuals. Sometimes individuals are separated because their illnesses could infect others. We call these acts of separation "quarantining."

A few weeks ago my computer caught a virus. Fortunately, after some investigative work, I realized what was happening. I downloaded an anti-virus software update and fixed the problem. But the software was unable to delete the infected file. Instead it somehow isolated it. In computer terminology, it "quarantined" the file, ensuring that it would not infect the other files on the computer.

In that case, quarantining was a good thing. But sometimes we try to quarantine the wrong things; we mix up our priorities. Like the walled cities of the Middle Ages whose security strategies backfired when they encountered the plague, we sometimes, in an effort to shore up our security, quarantine things of importance and allow things to run amok.

Paul Tillich, a famous twentieth-century theologian, described God as that which is of "ultimate concern," what is of most importance to each of us. The "ultimate concern" for many in Jesus' day seemed to be their religious rules and regulations. These had to be obeyed above all else. And anything that would draw them away from obeying the laws had to be quarantined. Those regulations were known as the "purity laws," and they did a good job at what they were designed to do—keep the Israelites set apart from others.

Jesus, however, saw how their laws had evolved to become their "ultimate concern," and he tried to correct the problem. But in so doing, he threatened the security the laws and traditions provided the people. So they tried to quarantine him, to isolate him so as not to infect the rest of their society. But Jesus could not be constrained by their restrictions. No walls could block his way. No anti-virus software could delete him or quarantine him. Instead, he continued to infect their society with a special kind of virus—an infection of mercy.

Jesus confronted their misguided perception of God and God's ways. He said it was not the people's religious rituals that were important, also not their purity laws, which, for example, forbade them from eating with tax collectors and sinners. What was important, rather, was showing mercy, showing compassion, to their fellow human beings. It wasn't that religion was unimportant. But when their rituals and their legalistic way of understanding their Scriptures became more important than showing mercy or compassion toward others, their laws had defeated their own purpose. They had quarantined themselves, together with a plague, behind high walls. Their "ultimate concern" became their tradition, and not God.

Of course, today we no longer have such archaic purity laws . . . or do we? I read this week about an Episcopal congregation that became bitterly divided. Two young women of the congregation had had babies out of wedlock about the same time. One put her baby up for adoption. The other decided, that with her parents' help, she could keep the child. Unfortunately, the congregation began taking sides as to which girl did "the most loving" thing. The division was intensified when the one girl wanted to have her baby baptized. Several members threatened to walk out if the priest agreed to honor her request. They said they would not have their church appear to sanction promiscuous activity. Their well-built walls were high.

But then there was a Presbyterian congregation who also had a young unwed mother. One Sunday morning the mother brought her newborn son to be baptized. Alone, she came down the isle to the baptismal font, in front of the pastor. As is their custom, the pastor asked the congregation, "Who stands with this child?" Hesitantly, the young girl's mother, sitting by herself at the side of the church, stood up. (Normally the entire congregation stands as well.)

Prepared for such a response, the pastor continued the service, but he was soon interrupted by some noise in the congregation. He looked up from his book and saw one of the patriarchs of the community standing up, and then his wife, and then a few other people here and there, until finally most of the congregation was standing with that small child (and his mother) for baptism—to welcome him into the household of God, the Body of Christ.

When Jesus called Matthew, the tax collector, one of the dregs of that society, to be his disciple, he didn't scold him or ask him to change. He didn't ask Matthew to act a certain way or believe certain things. Jesus simply said, "Follow me." And he loved him.

J. Michael Ehmer is vicar of St. Luke's Church,
Levelland, Texas.

Walking by the Spirit

Galatians 5:16–24
William Hethcock

THE APOSTLE PAUL has been patiently preaching the Gospel to the Gentiles, patiently writing letters to the newly formed congregations, and patiently seeing to the care of all the churches. Right now, however, the patient apostle is ticked off big-time with the Galatians.

"You foolish Galatians!" Paul wails. "It was before your eyes that Jesus Christ was publicly exhibited as crucified! You started with the Spirit," Paul reminds them, "but now you are ending with the flesh. What I want to know is who has bewitched you?"

Paul is angry about what has happened. He was there in their city. He gave them the Gospel firmly and clearly. He preached Jesus Christ crucified, and he preached so clearly that he left those Galatians ready to walk by the Spirit, the Spirit that was given to the world after Jesus' rising to new life.

But Paul has come to find out that things have gone wrong. After he left them, there arrived these ill-informed Jewish-Christian missionaries, who landed on the Galatians with a different message. They are changing the teaching Paul had given them when he was among them. These missionaries have been telling the new Gentile converts that they will not be true Christians until they have embraced the Hebrew traditions revealed by God in the ancient Law.

Paul is upset. How did he find out? Obviously, somebody snitched. Somebody, probably someone really excited, has written to Paul and told him all about it.

Paul, the most wonderful thing has happened! These missionaries, just recently converted to Christ themselves, have come to see us to give us the rest of the Gospel. We were sort of on our own without a lot of guidance. We had to think for ourselves and all. Well, Paul, these missionaries have told us the rest, the part you left out. Now we know all about the ancient Law that God gave his chosen people, and how if we obey the Law we can get to be righteous. Isn't that wonderful?

And they have told us about all the religious holidays and how to keep them. There's Purim and Pentecost and Passover and all the rest. And we have learned how to be really good Jews so that we may now become really good Christians.

And Paul, there's another thing, though it's a little indelicate to mention, but I'll tell you anyway. It's an important part of what's going on.

*The Gentile guys you converted here in Galatia are getting themselves cir-
cumcised. Even though it's minor surgery and the missionary surgeons are
used to operating, it has created a little inconvenience. You know, Paul,
ether hasn't been invented yet, but we have good wine. And a lot of very
good wine has been snarfed down by the fellahs. They just slap each other
on the back and say, "Well, what's a little ouch-ness in the name of the
Lord Christ."*

Paul is devastated. He planted the garden and left it flourishing, and
now someone has come in and planted weeds. And that's why he's firing
off this testy letter to the Galatians.

Why do you suppose the good Gentile-Christian converts in the
churches in Galatia would fall for this false understanding of the work of
Jesus Christ instead of what Paul had preached to them so plainly? He left
them striving to walk by the Spirit, and now they are walking by the flesh.
Why did it happen? Paul is heartbroken.

Actually, Paul knows why it happened, and I know why it happened,
and you know why it happened. *It's easier to walk by the flesh than it is
to walk by the Spirit.*

The Galatians have been duped into thinking they are free, and they are
not. They think they've discovered a shortcut to holiness, and they've
taken it. And what has Paul so outraged is that they like it better than the
true way, because walking the way of the flesh is so natural for them. They
don't even know they're not free.

It's easy to misunderstand walking by the Spirit. We do it all the time.
It's easy to misunderstand it because it's so scary. Walking by the flesh is
natural; we already know how to do it. It's part of us. Walking by the
Spirit requires faith. We have to trust the Spirit all the time, and not just
in spurts. For us children of the world, that gets tough.

Walking according to the flesh has a sense of security about it. Those
well-meaning missionaries brought a gospel that answered everyone's need
for rules and structure. They were teaching the Galatians to be Law-obser-
vant so that they could claim to be rooted in history, in the divine tradition
of God's people. A lot of the tough decisions were already made for them.

All these Gentile-Christians whom Paul had converted to the faith had
come to Jesus Christ from a background of worshiping pagan idols. Their
pagan formularies had explained everything. Their questions about the
world and where it was going had been answered. The answers had been
wrong in our God's terms, but they were answers nonetheless. With the
new version of Christ's Gospel learned from the Jewish-Christian missionaries, the people suddenly had firm guidelines again, and they believed
as people do that they needed guidelines to keep their world from falling
into chaos.

Under Paul's leadership, they had come to know the crucified and risen Christ. They had discovered themselves called to walk by the Spirit. When they began to walk by the Spirit in Paul's terms, they weren't guided by a whole lot of ready-made answers. They came to be guided instead by the Spirit's own self. They could neither hear nor see the Spirit, but they were learning through faith that the Spirit was guiding them in the difficult times and the tough calls. Things were never old hat; every day was exciting and new.

Walking by the Spirit, they were becoming a community of flexibility and freedom, living with openness toward the unpredictable movement of God's Spirit. They were being wonderfully freed up. They were experiencing the adventure of walking by the risky Spirit who is always out of control, always on the brink of something new, always daring a new direction. They began to mix with people to whom before becoming Christian they would not have given the time of day. They began through the Spirit to reach out to their pagan brothers and sisters and to tell them the good news of Jesus Christ. Walking in the Spirit, they were delighting in the promise that they were moving toward the kingdom of God, that they might even themselves enter into it, just as Paul had promised them in Christ's name.

But walking in the Spirit required faith; they had to trust all that Paul had said to them. And sometimes, especially when things were not going well, they were frightened and worried. Flesh would creep in. Faith alone kept them walking in the Spirit, and sometimes their faith wavered, just as does yours and mine.

Then came the missionaries. "You're working without a safety net, Galatians," they preached. "Here is the Law. It's beautiful, it's old, it's God-given, and it's a sure thing. And you've got to become a good Law-follower before you can enter into Christ."

"What a relief!" the Galatians said to one another. "Paul must have left something out. This is a lot easier than before."

And they never knew what was really happening—that they were giving up walking by the Spirit, and that they were taking on walking by the flesh as if it were something new and wonderful. No wonder Paul is heartbroken. The story breaks my heart; I am sure it breaks yours as well.

So I have to ask you: Is the church you came from to this conference walking by the Spirit? Being a seminarian is tricky, because you can suddenly be walking by the flesh and enjoying every minute of it. Alas, being ordained is no guaranteed remedy. *It's easier to walk by the flesh than it is to walk by the Spirit.* It's so comfortable because it is so normal, because we are so much of the world.

Paul says that if we are confused about whether we are walking in the flesh, there are some clues. Suddenly there are things like quarrels, dissensions among believing friends, factions instead of fellowship, bursts of uncontrolled anger, jealousy, and even a little too much Scotch. It's harder to tell when we're walking by the Spirit, but Paul says there are some hints there as well: love, joy, peace, patience, kindness, generosity, faithfulness, gentleness, self-control. I wonder, is your church walking by the Spirit?

Listening to Paul's letter to those Galatian-Christians reminds me that I am called by Christ Jesus to walk by the Spirit whom he has sent to be with me as I strive to be in Christ. I'm going to decide once again right now, even though I have made the decision many times before, to respond faithfully to that call. Will you join me? Together we may find ourselves with God's gracious help walking by the Spirit more and more every day.

William Hethcock is professor of homiletics, emeritus, The School of Theology, University of the South Sewanee, Tennessee. This sermon was delivered at the Preaching Excellence Conference.

Treasure in the Interplay of Old and New

Matthew 13:52
Feast of Ephrem of Edessa
Mark William Wastler

TODAY WE commemorate Ephrem of Edessa. What does the memory of a fourth-century hymn writer have to do with us, other than the fact that one of his hymns is in our hymnal?

This Gospel reading concludes a long teaching section in which Jesus uses a series of parables to explain the kingdom of heaven both to his disciples and to the crowds. It begins small, he tells them, and people respond to it differently. Its fullness is in the future. Judgment is an important part of it. At the conclusion of this long series of parables that the crowds seem not to understand, Jesus asks his friends, "Have you understood all this?" They say, "Yeah, we get it."

Jesus responds to their affirmation by telling them still another parable, one about *them*, and about the effect of this teaching in *their* lives. He says, "Every scribe who has been trained for the kingdom of heaven is like the master of a household who brings out of his treasure what is new and what is old."

"Scribe" in this case refers to these disciples who have learned from Jesus how to interpret the Law. He has taught them to connect the ancient heritage with the latest work of God in the world. When students of the Law are fully trained, or "discipled," they see and explain the relationship between God's work in the past and God's work in the present.

We expect this from Matthew. We expect the Jesus of Matthew's account to be interested in fulfilling the old, not discarding it. In chapter five, verse seventeen, Jesus says those familiar words, "Do not think that I have come to abolish the law or the prophets; I have come not to abolish but to fulfill." There is no surprise here.

Jesus' message to his disciples goes far beyond simply interpreting the Jewish Scriptures, however. He offers his friends a deep spiritual insight: the old things in life are just as valuable as the new. The new does not replace the old. Together they make a treasure.

This insight of Jesus' rings true for us. Think about your life in Christ. Think back to the early days of your faith, or to your first year of seminary. If you are like me, there are some things I thought, believed, and said in the early days of my faith that I wish I could forget. I made theological statements to the Commission on Ministry that cause me to wonder how I ever made it through the process. (There really is grace!)

When we put who we *have been* next to who we *are*, we find a treasure. The new next to the old shows the work God has done in our lives. You each bring to your current ministry and work all that you did before. Your pursuit of ordination does not mean you leave behind what you did before. Whether you worked for an international relief agency, had a psychiatry practice, or sold t-shirts in Key West, that work combines with your current calling, and together they form a treasure.

This insight from Jesus that the old and new form a treasure is important for our pastoral work. The first summer at my new parish as a recently ordained deacon, I visited as many people as I possibly could who were homebound or in nursing homes. One day I turned up at the door of an elderly lady. She greeted me warmly and ushered me to a seat in the living room. The chair looked comfortable, but I could have used another one nearby that looked hideously uncomfortable. The agony of that other chair would have helped me stay "pastorally present" on that warm afternoon, especially just after eating lunch.

As we sat eating our cookies and sipping tea, she told me stories about her children and her late husband, whom she adored. Suddenly it hit me. There were about thirty old pictures of her and her husband and family all around the room, and they were all pointed at this one chair. Her message was clear: I am old and new. There is more to me than the person sitting here with you. I am also that woman you see in the pictures. The treasure we call life is made of the past as well as the present. We do well to remember that as pastors.

Jesus' parable also provides some insight into the task of the preacher. "Every scribe who has been trained for the kingdom of heaven is like the master of a household who brings out of his treasure what is new and what is old." That is exactly what we do as preachers. We bring out the old and put it alongside the new. Together they form a treasure.

John Stott, the famous English evangelical preacher, wrote in his appropriately titled book, *Between Two Worlds: The Art of Preaching in the Twentieth Century,* "Our task [as preachers] is to enable God's revealed truth to flow out of the Scriptures into the lives of the men and women of today."[1] He says that we are bridge builders between the ancient texts and the modern world; between the truths of Scripture and the lives of individuals. We bring out the old and put it next to the new.

Climbing a mountain on a glacier is a lonely, isolating experience. Although there may be several other people on the expedition, during the course of a fourteen- or eighteen-hour day you spend very little time next to anyone. You are all tied into a rope, and there is about sixty feet of rope between one person and the next. The only interaction you have is shouting commands at one another. There is a technique to alleviate the isolation. During rest periods, one rope team stops, and the other one parallel parks next to it. This give you a chance to talk with someone tied into the same position on the other rope. Oftentimes you discuss the route so far, look at the map and see where you are going. Hopefully, your partner has better snacks than you do so you can share some food. The two come next to each other for strength, direction, and nourishment.

Preachers do the same thing between the ancient truths and the lived experience of our listeners. Connecting our experience with the past connects us with something greater than ourselves. We all want our lives to be part of something larger; we long for our story to be part of a bigger story. Advertisers know this to be true, and they manipulate that need in hopes that we might buy our way into the grand narrative of Life. But there is nothing that really meets that need except God.

That—at last—is why Ephrem of Odessa is important. Remembering Ephrem and his hymns connects us with the story of God's redemption that has been going on longer than we have been around. Remembering the ancient work of God helps us understand it in the ever-present now.

We are faced with no easy task. Between a world fascinated with the new and our historical amnesia as a society, Jesus' message sounds very radical. Valuing truth revealed in ancient documents is counter-cultural. The world yawns when we reach for an old text.

---

1. John R. W. Stott, *Between Two Worlds: The Art of Preaching in the Twentieth Century* (Grand Rapids, Michigan: William B. Eerdmans Publishing Company, 1982), 182.

We can hear the words of Proverbs, floating in the air as a quiet admonition, "My child, do not forget my teaching. . . ." As preachers we are called to connect contemporary life with the truth of the Scriptures. When we build those bridges, when we connect the old with the new, we bring forth God's treasure.

Mark William Wastler is rector of St. Margaret's Church, Annapolis, Maryland. This sermon was delivered at the Preaching Excellence Conference.

Acting Ourselves into Thinking Right

John 13:1–15
Maundy Thursday
Susan Sommer

WE SHARED the same first name, but that seemed to be all we had in common. I was twenty-three years old and as naive as they come. She was in her fifties, under no illusions about anything. We were on a parish committee together, planning a series of yearlong events to raise awareness around the subject of alcoholism. The area of Michigan where we lived had the highest per capita rate of alcoholism in the state. The committee had been earnestly discussing educational programs and materials. All this time, Sue was uncommonly quiet. Finally, the rector asked for her opinion. Blowing out a cloud of cigarette smoke, she said. "These programs are fine, but they ain't gonna get no one sober."

Several sets of eyebrows, including my own, shot up. "Look," she said, "take it from someone who's spent a lot more years drunk than sober. It's real hard to think yourself into acting right. A whole lotta stuff just gets in the way. Mostly, what you gotta do is act yourself into thinking right."

I remember struggling with Sue's observation. Surely any kind of change in one's life proceeds first from a careful analysis of facts. Get your head straight and the rest of you will follow. Isn't that how it works? How could she be right?

Well, as I said, I was naive. Turns out, she was right—not only about substance abuse, but about many other things as well, including our faith. When we talk about deep, gut-level conversion to an entirely new way of being, mostly what we gotta do is act ourselves into thinking right. It's the scandal of Maundy Thursday.

We just heard John's account of the Last Supper. Unlike Matthew, Mark, and Luke, John gives us no words of institution—no commemorating words over the bread and wine. Instead, we get the account of Jesus washing the feet of his scandalized disciples after supper was over. You've heard it before. I'll say it again: This was shocking behavior on Jesus' part. Hospitality in that part of the world included dinner guests having their feet washed. That part was expected. But the job was inevitably relegated to the household slave with the lowest possible status. The dinner host would command that the washing take place; but he would never do it. As for the guest of honor taking the responsibility, that was unthinkable. Little wonder Peter protested so vehemently.

But Jesus would not be dissuaded. And when he had finished and put his clothing back on again, he said to them, "If I, your Lord and Teacher, have washed your feet, you also ought to wash one another's feet. For I have set you an example, that you also should do as I have done to you." In a very short time, he would be put to death. He would no longer be with them as he had been. They had to grasp the love that he had been teaching them all this time, because they were the ones who were going to have to incarnate it. They were going to have to carry it forth into communities of faith they would eventually nurture in the name of their resurrected Savior. They would be proclaiming the good news of the love of God to an unloving world. The only way that any of it could make sense was for them to do as Jesus had done. The only way that they could ever think of themselves as servants of God was for them to act like servants of God right from the outset.

The Great Mandate of Maundy Thursday is that we should wash one another's feet. There are many implications in this image. Speaking from experience, I can assure you that it is an act of astonishing intimacy. I know that there are many of you who balk at the notion of having your feet washed. But it goes both ways. There are many people in this world whose feet we don't particularly want to wash, people whom we don't particularly want to love, people for whom we don't particularly want to be Christ, people in whom we don't particularly want to seek Christ. If I get that close, handle their very feet, so to speak, I can no longer ignore them. To wash another person's feet is to acknowledge a fundamental relationship and shared humanity. It's so much easier to stay in your head, to love the unlovely theoretically, naively hoping that someday maybe our actions will reflect our words and our beliefs. It's safer to try to think our way into acting right. That way, we're far less apt to be actually confronted by the full scandal of the Gospel.

Yet Jesus washes the feet of all twelve of his disciples, including the feet of Judas. John's Gospel tells us that Jesus knew who his betrayer was. And still he knelt at his feet and washed them too. His is a love that loves in the full knowledge of betrayal. Imagine that love set loose upon the world. Imagine a world acting in that kind of love.

Susan Sommer is vicar of Grace Church, New Lennox, Illinois.

OFFERING UNSETTLING INSIGHTS INTO FAMILIAR TEXTS

Crumbs

Matthew 15:21–28
Proper 15A
Sheila Nelson-McJilton

CRUMBS. That's all she is looking for. Crumbs. Not the whole loaf. Not even a slice. Just crumbs. Small crusty crumbs that fall over the edge of the table. And she knows that he can give her what she needs. She has heard about this Jewish messiah, Jesus of Nazareth. He turns clear, cool water into rich, red wine. He takes a few loaves and fishes from one boy and feeds thousands. Now he comes out to the borders of Palestine where she and her tormented daughter live on the edge of existence. It's been a long time since this woman has enjoyed a banquet. She has almost forgotten how to claim her place at the table. But she has heard about Jesus of Nazareth. She knows he has something from God to feed people. And she intends to get some of that something for her daughter. Crumbs. She will take crumbs, if that is all she can get.

We do not know what finally pushes the woman over the edge. The writer of Matthew does not tell us. Perhaps she sits at her empty table one day. Her house is small; the afternoon heat is unbearable. And then, her young daughter, seized by a fit, falls to the dirt floor in convulsions. The Gospel writer does not give us much background. We can only presume to imagine that this desperate woman has had enough. Suddenly, she pushes away from an empty table and runs out the door. Out the door and down the road. Desperate for crumbs. Then she sees Jesus of Nazareth.

It's interesting, isn't it? It seems that Jesus has had enough as well. He has had enough of rigid, hypocritical rules—what Matthew calls "the tradition of the elders." He has had enough of deaf, dumb disciples who stumble around blindly and just don't get it. Jesus leaves the cool waters of the Galilee to travel northwest on dusty roads. Out on the far edges of Israel. Out there on the border—figuratively and literally. "On the boundary between the old and the new, between male and female, between Jew and Gentile, between friend and enemy, between the holy and the demonic."[1]

It is here, on the edge of existence, where we see great faith. From somewhere deep inside her, this woman seizes that faith, strides out the door and down the dusty road. As she approaches Jesus of Nazareth, she starts shouting: "Have mercy on me, Lord, Son of David!" Shrieking. Screaming. Shouting. This word "shouting" used by the Gospel writer is the same word used in Revelation to describe the cries of a woman in labor pains. So, just as this woman once cried out as she gave birth to her daughter, she now cries out in a struggle to give health and wholeness to that child.

She knows that she, a Canaanite woman, with no better status than a dog, is not worthy to gather up the crumbs under the table. Yet she knows something about God's mercy that the Pharisees and scribes do not know. She knows something that even Jesus' disciples do not know. She knows that God's mercy is wide and broad and wonderfully kind and faithful and bountiful. God's divine love is even wider—even wider—than the love of the human Jesus of Nazareth. It is in this certain knowledge that the Canaanite woman dares to shout for God's mercy as she kneels in front of the human Jesus.

What does she get for her trouble? At first, nothing—except stony silence. Jesus ignores her, and the disciples probably roll their eyes. But when she continues to shout, the disciples are pushed over the edge. Get rid of this woman, Jesus. Send her away, will you? We had enough crazy people to deal with in Galilee, and they were our own kind. Now we've got crazy foreigners ranting and raving in the road. Do something. Do anything. Just get rid of her, okay? Enough already!

Jesus responds, but not to the woman kneeling before him. He ignores the woman and responds to the disciples. "I was sent only to the lost sheep of Israel," he says firmly. I know who I am. I am Israel's messiah. My own people sit in darkness and need to see a great light. I was sent to bring my own people healing, justice, mercy. I am a Jew—"the Jew who stands as the culmination of all of Israel's history."[2] Yes, and more than a messiah for Israel. The human and historic Jesus claims his identity as Israel's messiah. And yet this woman who lives on the edges, on the margins, claims even more than Jesus does himself, for she sees beyond the Jewish man in

---

1. Thomas Long, *Matthew* (Louisville: Westminster/John Knox Press, 1997), 174.
2. Ibid., 176.

front of her. Her vision extends back in history to the Davidic royal line, and forward in history to the crucified and risen Christ. This Jewish messiah before whom she kneels is a fulcrum for faith for thousands of people, those who live bountiful, mainstream lives and those who struggle for crumbs on the edges of life. Jesus is the messiah of Israel. And Jesus is the savior of the entire world.

The Pharisees and scribes may not get it. The disciples may not get it. But this poor Canaanite woman gets it. Jesus says, "It is not fair to take the children's food and throw it to the dogs." And the woman turns the metaphor back on him with sharp and sure retort. "Yes, Lord, yet even the dogs eat the crumbs that fall from their master's table." Here is the kind of fierce, ferocious faith that will transform a world. So out of a faith that persists and struggles, out of a faith that seizes and shouts for attention, the woman receives what she demands. Healing for her daughter. Mercy that is wide and broad and wonderfully kind and faithful and bountiful.

So what? What can this story possibly mean for us—we who did not experience the historical, human Jesus sent to save his own people? We baptized Christians have long since claimed our places at God's table. We have forgotten a first-century Jewish messiah even as we remember a crucified and risen Christ in the breaking of bread and in the prayers. We have long since claimed the banquet of gifts given by the power of the Holy Spirit. And we—well educated, upper middle class, wealthy in comparison to most of the world—have all, and more, than we need. We do not grovel for crumbs under anyone's table. Our lives are bountiful and rich.

Here is the sharp edge of this Gospel reading. Because we claim our places at God's table, as God's sons and daughters, we have claimed a place not only of privilege, but one of responsibility. This place requires us to feed our brothers and sisters. Crumbs. That's all they are looking for. Crumbs. Not the whole loaf. Not even a slice. Just crumbs. You and I want the whole loaf, of course, and we usually get it. We drive SUVs. They take buses or the subway, or they walk. We have pension plans. They lack basic health insurance so they must bring crying babies to the emergency room at midnight. We have two-hundred-thousand-dollar homes with two-car garages. They live in crowded, noisy apartments. We get regular paychecks. They cannot keep jobs because too many of them slept last night in a shelter. They were kept awake by snoring. An uncomfortable cot. The wailing of hungry babies. And when you fall asleep on the job, you don't have a job for long.

Crumbs. They want more than crumbs because deep in their souls, they know they deserve more. And yet they often do not know who to ask or how to ask. So they wait. They wait in emergency rooms and welfare lines. They wait in line for sandwiches and coffee in MacPherson Square in Washington, D.C. They bus tables or they serve tables, but we do not let them pull up a chair and eat at that table. Some of them are tired of waiting. Angry at waiting. So they get high or drunk and rob convenience stores. They kidnap little girls or rape women and leave their bodies in parks. They strap bombs on their bodies, walk onto crowded buses, and blow themselves up.

The people who live out there on the edges of life are sick to death of waiting for the banquet to begin, so they stand in front of us and demand crumbs. The crucified, risen, and ascended Christ asks: When will you feed them? When will you help them learn to read? When will you join Habitat for Humanity and help them build a home? When will you work for justice so there will be peace? When will you look them in the eye and say, "Thank you for being my waiter today. You did a good job"?

Yes, there's a wideness in God's mercy. Two thousand years ago, a Canaanite woman knew this. God gave her clarity of vision so that she saw far beyond the edge of her empty table to a banquet table. She knew that God's banquet table is full and that any crumb from that table would fill her. Way down that dusty road, even beyond the human vision of Jesus of Nazareth, the divine plan of God would feed the whole world, not just part of the world.

The banquet waits for each one of us. Not simply because a Jewish messiah walked the roads of Palestine, but because of Jesus of Nazareth, who died on a cross and rose from a tomb. It is the risen Christ who feeds us, who calls us to feed others in the power of the Spirit. None of God's children have to gather crumbs under the table, because it is the property of God always to have mercy. In Christ and through Christ, we are all worthy to come to God's banquet table, and no one gets crumbs here. God's table is full of big, crusty, homemade loaves of bread. It is full of rich, red wine. The gifts of God. For the people of God. Take them in remembrance that Christ died—and rose—for you. And be thankful.

*Sheila Nelson-McJilton is associate rector of Christ Church,
Stevensville, Maryland. This sermon was delivered at the
Preaching Excellence Conference, and received the fourth
annual John Hines Preaching Award from Virginia Seminary.*

Primal Faith

Matthew 15:21–28
Proper 15 A
Pamela S. Morgan

HOW DESPERATE would you have to be to ask for help from a god you did not know? How desperate would you have to be to approach the god of another faith? As Christians and Anglicans, we believe we can ask the saints to help us by praying for us from their nearer presence to God. That's a common intercession, well within our own faith.

There was a time when I was senior warden at St. Matthew's Episcopal Church in Benton, Arkansas. The vicar had lost some important paperwork. When he called to tell me, he was nearly frantic. I asked him if he requested the prayers of St. Anthony, patron saint of the lost. He said, "I've asked Anthony and all the rest of the saints. If I don't find it in the next thirty minutes, I'm going to ask the Buddha!" You might say it's a desperate moment when Episcopal priests seek help from the Buddha.

This is the kind of desperate plea the Canaanite woman made to Jesus on behalf of her daughter. Straight away, the disciples recognized the woman from the region of Tyre and Sidon as an enemy. Tyre and Sidon had been enemies with Israel ever since the reign of Ahab and Jezebel. All of the characters in this Gospel scene, even the Canaanite, would have been familiar with Ezekiel's prophesy, and with how God confronted Tyre and Sidon for the way they had mistreated the Israelites.

They bought Hebrew slaves, then sold them to Gentile families deep within their own region. So there actually were Israelites enslaved in Tyre and Sidon. That's why Jesus responded as he did to his disciples' request that he send the worrisome woman away: "I was sent into this enemy territory to find those lost sheep of Israel and liberate them."

Now there was a time (when the nation of Israel was united under the reign of David) that Israel and Tyre enjoyed a good relationship as neighboring nations. In the woman's address of Jesus as "son of David," she was appealing to that time of good relationship. Her sincerity was evident when she threw herself at his feet. It was even more evident in what she said. For in essence she said, "We'd rather be tame dogs serving our master in the house of Israel than enemies outside it."

You see, the Canaanite woman's faith was not in Jesus as God's Messiah promised through the prophets to restore Israel, or the Savior who would, by his own death, atone for the sins of the world. If she had believed these things about Jesus, that would have made it into the story, but there's no mention of it. Yet Jesus said to her, "How great is your faith."

Canaanites placed their faith in their kings. They believed the kings were endowed with wisdom and understanding superior to most humans. If King David could keep his kingdom whole and healthy, maybe the descendant of David, a man with the reputation of a prophet, a prophet with healing power—maybe such a man could bring health and wholeness to her daughter. The faith Jesus found so commendable was her belief in the possibility that he, a Jew, could or would intervene in her life (she being an enemy of Jews) and free her daughter from the demon.

We confess our faith in the words of the Nicene Creed. We need those words to understand our faith as Christians and especially to talk about it. But the existence of faith is not dependent upon our understanding it. Faith, at its primal level, lies far beneath the words we use to speak of it. It knows none of the religious distinctions that our minds know. Faith in its essence is neither Christian, nor Jewish, nor Muslim, nor Buddhist, nor Hindu, nor anything else. These are names for faith, avenues for faith, structures for the expression of faith. But faith in its most primitive form just is.

I saw this primal faith once when I was chaplain at the University of Arkansas for Medical Sciences. I had just finished the Sunday morning worship service when a woman came in and asked if I would pray with her. She said to me, "I am not a Christian." I said, "I'd be happy to pray with you, but I only know how to pray as a Christian."

She went on to say, "My husband has multiple myeloma. We are here for a bone marrow transplant." Then she began to cry. She said, "We have been here for many weeks. I miss my family. It's too far for them to come. My husband is so sick, and I'm afraid he won't recover. I don't know where to go to find someone to pray in the way I know. Will you please pray to your Christian God that the treatment will work and I can have my husband well so we can go home to our family?" I said, "Certainly."

And I prayed to our God for her husband and for her.

When I reflected on what happened with the woman in the chapel, I was amazed and humbled that the woman, desperate to have her husband's health and their lives restored, was willing to approach a god she did not know for help. Her faith, like the Canaanite's, was not bound by religious, ethnic, or political constraints. It was a bare-bones kind of faith. Faith that reached across those boundaries to claim the possibility that a daughter or a husband would be healed.

We Christians have a name for our faith. We have a structure, a way to understand our faith, a way to express ourselves. We're comfortable, and our faith works for us. But what if we find ourselves in a desperate situation? Someone we love is so sick we're afraid he won't recover. Someone we love needs liberation from addiction, abuse, or indebtedness, and needs it now. Someone we love dies unexpectedly and suddenly the structure of our faith is not strong enough to support us. The creed seems hollow. Understanding our faith and talking about it doesn't bring us comfort. There's an ache in our gut that helps us cry out to whatever god is listening in the same way an infant cries for food and takes milk from anyone who offers it.

If this happens to us Christians with our well-developed faith, does it mean we've lost it? Have we denied it in some way? Has our faith betrayed us? Or forsaken us? No. In those desperate times our primal faith, the faith Jesus acknowledged in the Canaanite woman, comes to our aid.

Wearing the name of Christian doesn't insure us against those desperate moments in our lives, but it does assure us who hears our cries for help. Because we belong to Christ, he intercepts our cries in the air and makes them perfect in the ear of our God.

Pamela S. Morgan is curate of St. Mark's Church,
Little Rock, Arkansas.

Naming the Way of the World
Matthew 25:14–15, 19–29
Proper 28 A
Kit Carlson

"FOR TO ALL those who have, more will be given, and they will have an abundance. But from those who have nothing, even what they have will be taken away." Ain't it the truth? The rich get richer and the poor get poorer. It's the way of the world. It is a way that Jesus wants us to examine closely in this parable of the talents.

You see, this parable is not about "talents," not the way we think of talented people or specific talents God has given us, like a talent for singing or a talent for tennis, or gifted and talented children. It's not even a parable about the Kingdom of God . . . there's no Kingdom language in here, and I don't think any one of us wants to think of God as a "harsh master." No, this is a parable about the world, the world as it actually was in Jesus' time and the world as it is today.

As Jesus tells this parable, sitting on the porch of the Temple in Jerusalem, his audience immediately recognizes the master. This is the head of a great household, the closest thing in the ancient world to a blue-chip corporation. This is a man of phenomenal wealth. Look at what he doles out to his slaves. In that world, a talent was a unit of money, worth about fifteen years' worth of wages. A conservative estimate of what the master entrusts to his slaves is about 2.5 million dollars.

Then the audience learns that this master is also an absentee landlord, a common and despised feature of life in first-century Palestine. Such landowners got rich by loaning money to small farmers. When the crops failed and the farmers couldn't pay, the lender got their land. Then he would hire them back to work on what had once been their family farms, at typical subsistence-level wages. So when Jesus introduces this powerful master, you can almost hear the booing from the crowd.

Next, Jesus introduces two more villains: the slaves who turn five talents into ten, and two talents into four. Now what, we might wonder, is wrong with that? Surely they were just good capitalists, taking those investments and making them grow. If only we could get return on our money like that in these days of sliding stock values, eh?

But there was no such thing as capitalism in the ancient world. There were no stock markets, no IPOs, no bonds or mutual funds. In the ancient world, wealth was seen as a limited resource. You couldn't grow more of it. So the only way to make vast sums of money would be to take it away from someone else, typically by charging interest on loans, or by extortion, or fraud. More booing, no doubt, ensues from Jesus' listeners when he describes these fellows.

Finally, Jesus presents the hero of the story, the slave who refuses to participate. He does not join his fellows in exploiting poor people on the master's behalf. He does not "go along to get along." No, he boycotts the system. He takes his talent out of circulation and presents it undivided but also undeveloped to the master on his return. Then the slave has the gall to speak truth to this powerful man, to call him "harsh," to point out that the master makes his wealth not from his own labors, but from the labors of others. And like so many whistle-blowers and rabble-rousers before him and since, the slave gets stripped of what little he has and tossed out on his ear.[1]

---

1. I am indebted for this interpretation to Ched Myers and Eric de Bode and their article, "Towering Trees and 'Talented' Slaves," from *The Other Side*, May-June 1999, vol. 35, no. 3. Several commentaries also mentioned Bruce Malina's *The New Testament World: Insights from Cultural Anthropology* as a source for understanding the ancient world's perspective on wealth as a limited resource.

"For to all those who have, more will be given and they will have an abundance. But from those who have nothing, even what they have will be taken away." Ain't it just the truth? The rich get richer and the poor get poorer. All the folks listening to Jesus would have nodded their heads in sympathy and comprehension. That's how it is, all right. No kidding. You tell it, Jesus.

And those of us listening today can nod our heads right along with them. The world hasn't changed all that much since the year 33 C.E. The rich still get richer. The more you have, the more you seem to be able to get. It doesn't mean you're evil or fraudulent. If you have, it's easy to get more. Just ask those who've refinanced their mortgages at these shockingly low interest rates. You can pay off debt, get cash to pay for college or home improvements, and still end up with a lower monthly mortgage payment. It's amazing how much one house can get you these days.

But find a man who's living paycheck to paycheck. Maybe he's got a few medical bills and can't make the car payment. He loses the car and can't keep his job. Without the job, he can't pay the rent. The next thing you know, he's down in Rockville at the Community Based Shelter trying to put the whole house of cards back together again. He had nothing to start with, or close to it, and what little he had was taken away.

And that's the way of the world, the whole wide world. This is a world where only fifteen percent of the population accounts for seventy-eight percent of global consumption. It's a world where seventy percent of the poor are female, where one hundred sixty million children are malnourished. It's a world where more than eight hundred million people are hungry, and that includes thirty-one million people right here in the United States. It is a world where one out of every five people lives on less than one dollar a day.

But it is also a world where there is plenty for all. It's just that those who have much keep getting more and those who have little keep losing theirs. For instance, there is enough food in the world right now for every single person to get more than the twenty-three hundred calories a day they need to thrive. It is a world where, with just forty billion dollars, there could be universal access to education for all children, universal access to fresh water and sanitation for every person on the planet. Microsoft chairman Bill Gates could cover that entire cost himself, and he would still have a net worth of 12.5 *billion* dollars.

Now I am not naïve enough to believe that just the waving of a hand, even the hand of Bill Gates, will solve hunger, homelessness, disease, and despair in the world. There are wars and famines and corrupt governments and international debts and dictators and guerrilla armies and addictions and monsoons and any number of things that make healing a broken world hard, hard work. But this is the very work to which we are called, and this parable points us to the reason why.

This parable is crucial to our understanding of who Jesus is and where he is calling us to go. It's crucial, because, as Matthew presents it, this is one of the three final parables that Jesus tells before he heads off to the Last Supper and then to the cross. This is part of the very last teaching Jesus gives his disciples, and us, before he dies.

Last week, we heard the first of the three parables, the one about the wise and foolish bridesmaids, and we were told to stay awake! Because Jesus is coming soon, and we need to be ready to meet him when he arrives. Now, this week, we get this very earthly parable that outlines the eternal truism that the rich get richer and the poor get poorer. Then, like a three-part joke, we have to wait for next week to get the punch line. Next week, we hear the parable of the sheep and the goats. And the parable of the sheep and goats reminds us that if we are looking for Jesus, we will find him when we see someone who is hungry or thirsty or a stranger or naked or sick or in prison—when we see someone like that and care for him.

Together, these three parables form a three-part instruction manual for those of us who would follow this Jesus, the Christ who was and who is, and who is to come. One: Wake up and watch for Jesus. Two: Realize that we live in a world that privileges the rich and persecutes the poor. Three: Go to where you know Jesus will be.

You will not find him turning profits for an absentee landlord. You will not find him trading among the rich or the powerful. You will not find him dictating geopolitical decisions in the White House. You will not find him dining at The Palm. You will find him where there is wailing and gnashing of teeth, there in the outer darkness with the rebellious slave. You will find him among the poor, the dispossessed, and the destitute.

When we wake up and go looking for Jesus in this harsh and unjust world, we know how to recognize him. He will be hungry. He will be thirsty. He will be like a stranger come amongst us. He will be naked or in rags. He will be sick. He will be behind bars.

Jesus is waiting for us right now, waiting for us to come and give him good food, clean water, fresh clothes, affordable medicines, and simple companionship. He is waiting for us right now, in every hungry belly, in every outstretched hand, in every aching wound.

He is waiting for us now, trusting that we will see that the rule of his Kingdom is not that "the rich get richer and the poor get poorer."
It is to "love your neighbor as yourself."

Kit Carlson is associate rector of the Church of the Ascension, Gaithersburg, Maryland.

REORIENTING THE FAITH COMMUNITY TOWARD RESURRECTION LIFE

Easter Fear

Genesis 1:1–2:2; Exodus 14:10–15:1;
Ezekiel 37:1–14; Matthew 28:1–10
The Great Vigil of Easter
David J. Schlafer

HAVE YOU ever been *really afraid*? (Silly question! Everyone gets frightened now and then.) What is the *feeling* of fear? Is it for you as it is for me? My heart races and pounds. My mouth gets dry, my palms get wet. Shivers of electricity surge through my body. If I don't *draw* my breath—intentionally, deliberately—I feel like I will *lose* it.

But have you ever noticed? Fear is not simply a matter of "more or less." It comes in a wide variety of flavors.

Some fears are not so bad: *You made me jump! It's gonna be a wild ride! What a scary movie!*

Some fears can be very bad indeed: *Here it comes! Danger! We're not safe anymore!*

Some fears are closely wrapped with what we deeply care about: *I don't want to lose you! I'm not sure I can do it! It's risky, but I have to follow my bliss!*

There is one thing these fears have in common, however—the feeling of being out of control, of shooting down a rushing river in a small canoe without a paddle.

Easter is a frightening place in which to find yourself. We celebrate a day called Easter in the season of spring, but Easter and spring are not the same. Spring is a pleasant, predictable period to which we look forward. Easter is an earthquake that comes crashing in rudely when we least expect it.

In spring folks say: "Oh, how lovely!" On Easter they say: "Oh, my God!"

If you don't believe that, ask the soldiers who are doing guard detail in front of a dead man's tomb. As an assignment, what a drag! Utterly unexciting—no medals to be won, no promotions to be gained. But an essential mission for the purposes of international security, nonetheless. And orders are orders, if you are a soldier.

These guards are men who have been trained to deal with fear, whose job involves controlling by fear. It is their task to *put* the fear of Caesar-God into anybody who would even think of disobeying him.

But nothing in their training has prepared them for an encounter with an earthquake called Easter. The earth erupts. An angel descends, rolls away a giant stone, and plunks himself upon it.

"You don't mind if I sit here, do you, boys?" says the angel, brushing a bit of earthquake dust from the tip of a wing. Down go the guards like dominos, fainted dead away.

Now, notice what the angel does *not* say to the terrified soldiers. The angel does not say: "Fear not!" The angel does not say, "Oh, pardon me, I didn't mean to frighten you! Not to worry, I'm just an angel of the Lord. I wouldn't dream of distracting you from your duty watch. Here. Peace. Have an Easter egg."

No. The angel leaves them in a dead faint right where they are lying.

Why?

Perhaps he figures these guys might benefit from a dose of medicine that tastes a tad like their own.

There are others, however, in this Easter place who also find themselves overwhelmed—some women. These women are accustomed not to *imposing* fear on others, but to *living* in fear themselves. The angel meets these folks as well. Notice, again, what the angel does *not* say: "It's all right; nothing to be afraid of."

Instead, the angel issues them an almost military-sounding order: "Do not be afraid! Come and see. Then go and tell. That is my message. Now—move out!"

They follow the order as best they can. They have a look and head down the road. In joy. And still in fear.

When the God who made the world wonderful steps into the mess the world has made of itself—steps in and makes a move to set it right—when God gets good and ready to Easter us, our natural, inevitable, spontaneous response is fear.

Ask the children of Israel, standing at the edge of the Red Sea. *We'd rather live as slaves than die in the desert. Freedom sounds great when you're cringing under the crack of a cruel whip, but a journey into freedom— that is terrifying!*

Ask Ezekiel, grieving in a valley of dry bones, a battlefield of senseless slaughter. Ask him—*"Ezekiel! Can these bones live?"*

Ask Israelis, Palestinians. Ask embittered Irish Protestants, embittered Irish Catholics. Ask followers of Osama bin Laden and George W. Bush. *Can these bones live?*

And every single one of them and every single one of us stop, swallow hard, shake our heads, and say, just like Ezekiel does: *"I just don't know. For the life of me, I can't see how. Who wants war, really? But who trusts peace, really? Isn't stealing what peace we can by brandishing the threat of war our only option?"*

Then the God of Easter thunders: *Enough! Dry bones: Listen up! You shall live!*

Easter, you see, is not just a charming springtime story about a God who brings a good guy named Jesus back to life after a bunch of bad guys killed him dead. Easter is God's Great *No* to all the ways we threaten one another and do each other in.

"Prophesy to the bones," God tells Ezekiel. "Call in the wind of my spirit and bring them to life."

I am guessing that, when Ezekiel gets his orders, he is absolutely terrified. Do you realize what is going to happen when his word—God's word—comes true? All those folks who have killed each other in the valley of dry bones are going to come to life. And, once they do, they are going to have to learn to *live* with each other. (That's a much harder thing to learn than how to be the death of one another.)

God, you see, pronounces the last word on death: *It's over, folks. Now, LIVE with that!* Terrifying, isn't it?

So I have sympathy for the women who come and see an empty tomb, then leave to tell about it—joy, yes, and deep, deep fear as well. But right in the middle of their absolutely impossible journey, suddenly someone joins them: *"Greetings! I am here. Do not be afraid."*

When those words come from the Risen Christ, they don't sound like an impossible order, do they? They sound more like an invitation—and a promise. An invitation we simply cannot refuse; and a promise that, accepting the invitation, we cannot lose.

"Time and time again," Jesus tells his followers, *"as you carry word of God's Easter into the valley of dry bones, I will be there with you—for you."*

Fear is a fact, all right, but so is courage. Fear is not something we have to cower under. In God's Easter, fear explodes into boundless, surging, healing joy.

It would be nice if, by pouring water over Susan, Sarah, and Alyssa, we could coat them with a magic potion to protect them from every fear. Baptism does not do that. What baptism *does* do is bring them into a community of God-fearing folk who promise to love them, to be with them, and to hold their hands when they find themselves afraid.

Tonight we baptize Susan, Sarah, Alyssa, into the pounding heartbeat of healthy, holy Easter Fear. Do you hear it? It surges and pulses like this: *Neither death, nor life, nor principalities, nor powers, nor things present, nor things to come, nor height, nor depth, nor anything else in all creation will be able to separate us from the love of God in Jesus Christ our Risen Lord. Alleluia.*

David J. Schlafer is co-editor of this volume.

Re-Creating Fire

The Great Vigil of Easter
Cirritta Park

METAPHORS. They are the building blocks of our understanding of emotion, thought, and faith. It is so much easier to relate to someone else's experience when they describe a difficult walk by saying, "It was like slogging through a marsh" than by saying, "It was muddy." The metaphor gives you an instant picture of the person's journey and an insight into his or her thoughts and feelings.

Given the power of metaphor, is there any wonder the early Church set the celebration of Jesus' resurrection on the first Sunday after the first full moon after the vernal equinox? Spring is nature's most obvious metaphor for resurrection. All around are signs of new life—crocus, hyacinth, those light green shoots peeking from seemingly lifeless branches. Soon we'll see the redbug and the azalea blossom, followed by pink and white dogwood flowers. Winter's cold death gives way to spring's renewal of life and re-creation of earth.

Yes, it is easy to think of spring as an Easter metaphor. Yet, in half the world, Easter comes as summer fades and autumn colors herald the beginning of shorter days and darker skies. Easter comes to the Southern Hemisphere in the fall.

How does one face the onset of winter and simultaneously celebrate Easter? How do you sing the Exsultet in Queensland, Australia? What metaphor do these Christians have? I asked this question of a business colleague who lives in Brisbane. I wanted to know what metaphors they use Down Under during Eastertide.

The answer surprised me. Jane told me that one of the autumnal rituals of the Aboriginal people is to make fertile the agricultural fields, preparing them for next year's crops. This is a ritual that connects the people, the fields, the kangaroos, the cattle, and sheep so delicately that if any come out of balance, much devastation would occur on this continent-country. Unlike our farmers, who disc and turn over the soil each fall, the Aboriginal tribesman set everything on fire.

According to my colleague, there are many indigenous crops that open in the heat of the fire and, when the seed drops to the ground, flourish in the ash that serves as fertilizer. From the ashes, new life appears. This phenomenon happens in the United States—the fires in Yellowstone come to mind. But here, it is not usually planned. There, it is a part of the cycle of life.

Imagine! We're not talking about life emerging from dormancy—a feigned sleeplike death. This really is life coming from the midst of death. This is light that follows darkness and renders it powerless. The Divine creates light out of the ashes, renews the land, and provides sustenance for the people.

The more I reflect on this fire ritual of Australia's indigenous people, the more I like this metaphor for Easter's message better than the buds of spring. As I walk through my faith journey, I need to know that there is hope awaiting me in the dark times of my life. As I stand in my usually self-made ash pit, the image of God's power creating life in me comforts and calms my soul.

We started Lent in ashes, remember. Our foreheads smeared with the remainders of palms of old, we were reminded that we were dust and to dust we would return. I've often been depressed hearing those words, but no longer. Now, I know that God is in the ashes, calling me to re-create myself in Lenten reflections. Lent's ashes are no longer a reminder of my mortality but a harbinger of my new life to come. Easter's promise is that life comes from ashes. God, right now, is creating light from our darkest moments, even the darkness of the grave.

Many of you are familiar with the phrase "dark night of the soul." We use that phrase most often when we feel powerless over our life circumstances. Of course, there are other metaphoric descriptors for these difficult journeys: "mid-life crisis," "between job opportunities," "relationship transition," "down and out." Jesus would have called it Holy Saturday.

Holy Saturday. The day Jesus is dead, in the darkness of the tomb. There seems to be no hope. The disciples are in hiding, afraid of what has been and not knowing where to go next. During our dark times, we forget that the darkness and ashes are God's fallow ground.

We, too, are like the disciples, afraid to move and unsure of what to do next. We need to tap into the creative power of God that surrounds us in these moments, to connect to God's power within us. The dark times are our opportunity to partner with God in co-creating our new life and sharing that with others.

I've thought often over the last six months that our nation has been caught up in a Holy Saturday experience. September 11 was a Good Friday. Our way of life shattered, our expectations of the future abruptly rearranged, we've lived for half a year in a Holy Saturday world, an ash pit that we could feel and see.

Slowly, we are making our way out of the darkness. The recent memorial of light provides a visual reminder that light does come from the ashes. Thank God for artists and poets, who leashed their creative spirits to the Divine to give us a vision of hope! Seeing those columns of light rise where the twin towers of the World Trade Center once stood reminded all of us that, while we must live in darkness sometimes, God is in the midst of us.

To God, "the night and the day are both alike," as the hymn reminds us.

God was and is and will be present in the dark times of our souls. From the darkness God invites us to cling to Divine creativity and re-make our lives. God invites us into a partner relationship, not a parent/child relationship, to bring light to the world.

That's what brings us together on this Easter Eve. We've lit a new fire. We've heard the stories of God's saving power throughout the ages. We've heard the song that praises the new light piercing the darkness. We gather to share a holy meal as the Body of Christ.

The fire ushers the light of Christ into your being. The Divine lives in you and in the union that is made when you consume Bread and Wine. The promise of light and life is ready to spring from the ashes of your life journey. *This* is Easter. Christ is risen indeed. Alleluia.

Ciritta Park, CAE, is deacon at St. Paul's Church, Columbus, Ohio.

Take a Tambourine!

Exodus 14:10–14, 21–25; 15:20–21; Acts 10:34–43; John 20:1–18
Easter Day – Year A
Larry R. Benfield

TAKE ONE TAMBOURINE. Add a woman crying out in delirious joy. Throw in fifty more women dancing and twirling in a frenzy of jubilation. If you want to know what resurrection might look like, that is as good an image as any. Today is Easter Day, the day to talk about life overcoming death, about joy overcoming fear, and this day we will focus on something other than an empty tomb.

Here is why. People avoid tombs, empty or otherwise. Graveyards are serious, solemn places. When I was a child, I found myself always walking a bit faster when I went by the graveyard that was a couple of blocks from my house. I was afraid.

For many years in this country, with its history of Great Awakenings and revivals, and throughout medieval Europe, for that matter, with its repeated plagues, the story of God as lived out in the life of Jesus has been a story that has theologically emphasized the empty tomb and popularly emphasized avoiding the evils of this world and hell in the next world. For good or for ill, people have learned to distance themselves, and salvation and wholeness have became individualized.

Today I want us to take from this place a new image of resurrection, an image toward which we will want to run, an image that gathers us together. And the image of women in the dance, tambourines in hand, exultantly singing, is as good an image as any.

In fact, it is one of the earliest images in the Bible of our response to the power of goodness to transform us. In our first lesson today we read of the Israelites' journey through the Red Sea, a journey away from slavery on the west bank and into a new freedom on the east. Some scholars think that the earliest words of the Hebrew Bible ever put down on paper were the following, "And the prophet Miriam, Aaron's sister, took a tambourine in her hand, and all the women went out after her with tambourines and with dancing. And Miriam sang to them: 'Sing to the Lord, for he has triumphed gloriously; horse and rider he has thrown into the sea.'" That's a sight worth seeing, a song worth hearing.

These women were so excited that they danced and sang when they recognized resurrection in their midst. Yes, resurrection in its own way could come to people before 33 C.E. Resurrection was a brand new way to look at life. Resurrection was something the Israelite women would celebrate, not run from. Their fears had previously consumed them to the point that they wanted to return to slavery. Then they discovered God had delivered them from death to life. They didn't have to be slaves any longer. No empty tomb for them, just old slaveries left behind, a dance and a song to replace them.

In the Christian Testament we get a similar experience. If you carefully read in today's selection from the Acts of the Apostles what Peter had to say about Jesus' resurrection, you will notice that he says that God raised Jesus, but he does not focus on an empty tomb or even mention it. Peter focuses on how the resurrected Jesus is seen, not on where he once was.

And then there is the Gospel, the women leaving the tomb in fear and great joy. When they see Jesus, he tells them to tell his brothers where he will be seen, not where he is absent. The empty tomb fades in significance.

Now, here is why I want us to picture those women dancing as the symbol of our Easter feast instead of focusing on that tomb. First, as I said earlier, we avoid tombs, and I never want us to avoid the risen Christ by concentrating on where he is not. Second, an emphasis on that physical tomb outside the ancient walls of Jerusalem has the potential to tie the resurrected Christ to first-century Palestine, and I refuse to turn Christ into an historical artifact that shows up on some sort of National Geographic map. Third, and perhaps most important of all, central to resurrection is that it is a state of overcoming fear, and in its presence the joy of freedom replaces enslavement. Dancing and singing are vivid reminders in any age of that liberation.

"Do not be afraid." That sentence is repeated three times in today's readings from Exodus and Matthew's Gospel. If we want to know what resurrection can look like in our own lives, then imagine what it would be like if we no longer feared anything—if we did not fear for our financial security, or fear rejection by our friends or family or significant other, or fear growing old and being left alone. What if those things no longer enslaved us? What if the church stopped fearing its call to be as open in its love as Jesus was in his, if it stopped fearing the poor and the homeless and the doubting? If those fears start being discarded, I can assure you that the world will have its biggest experience with resurrection since the day of the two Marys running toward Jerusalem with the good news that Jesus lives.

Their maternal ancestors, standing on the east side of the Red Sea, stopped fearing what the Egyptians could do to them, were resurrected, and went on to form a kingdom. The women at the tomb stopped fearing that physical death was the absolute end to everything, were resurrected, and went on to form a church that has lasted for two thousand years. If we can stop fearing that our own lives are without meaning, we will be resurrected as this generation's members of the body of Christ, and there is no telling what God will be able to do through us. Stay at an empty tomb if you wish, but I want to go see where the body of Christ is: feeding the hungry, clothing the naked, giving sight to the blind, declaring justice to the oppressed, showing mercy to the outcast, bringing healing to all of us who toss and turn in fear and hurt each night. Resurrection has concrete consequences.

I want resurrection to be a current reality for us, not an historical artifact from the year 33 C.E. or merely a vague future hope. I want every one of us to leave our fears in the tomb and run toward where Christ is now living. I want all of us to be excited about the truth that nothing will over-come God's love. I want it to change people's lives. That is reason enough to dance with jubilation.

Take a tambourine. Add a woman crying out in delirious joy. Throw in fifty more women dancing and twirling in a frenzy of jubilation. If you want to know what resurrection looks like, that is as good an image as any. Take it home with you. Dance the dance yourself. Sing the song. It will change your life, and when it does, the world will never be the same again. That is why God raised Jesus from the dead.

Larry R. Benfield is rector of Christ Church, Little Rock, Arkansas.

■ 3

Preaching Paul Prophetically

A. Katherine Grieb

Introduction:
The Prophetic Task of Preaching and the Apostle Paul

The title I have chosen, "Preaching Paul Prophetically," summarizes my conviction that Paul of Tarsus, the historical first-century pastor of early Christian churches, may have a great deal to do with prophetic preaching in our own time. I will attempt to demonstrate this connection in several distinct steps. In the first half of the essay, I shall recall to memory the biblical paradigm of the seer and prophet as God's antidote to the sins of royal materialism and militarism. The stories of Samuel, Elijah, and Michaiah ben Imlah are especially helpful here, though we could just as well have used Isaiah of Jerusalem, Amos, Nathan, or Jeremiah. Then, I shall show how Fred Craddock's recommendation that preachers follow the form of the biblical text in our preaching of it might, in the case of the pastor-preacher Paul, be fruitfully extended to the project of following the example of this biblical pastor in our own preaching style.

In the second half of the essay, the biblical paradigm of the prophet is combined with the pastor-preacher Paul. First, I shall argue that in Paul's self-understanding, as we are able to retrieve it from his letters, the usual forced contrast between "pastor" and "prophet" breaks down completely. Paul, like Jesus before him, seems to have understood himself as standing within Israel's prophetic tradition as he pastored his fledgling Christian churches. Second, I shall describe some features of the way Paul relates the pastoral and prophetic tasks in his own "preaching," since Paul's letters were designed to be read aloud and performed as sermons. The task of the prophet-pastor is both "conservative" and "radical"; it is both "communal" and "solitary." Finally, with the help of Paul, I shall describe some of the temptations and spiritual dangers associated with the task of pastoral-prophetic preaching and recommend some spiritual disciplines that prophet-pastor preachers-in-training might usefully adopt.

1. The Prophetic Paradigm in Israel's History and Today

In a recent sermon, "Taking Up the Cross in a Time of War," Matthew Gunter reflects:

I saw a woman wearing a t-shirt last summer that I found very troubling and very telling. It was a white t-shirt that had JESUSAVES written across the front. I believe he does. But that was not the only message on the shirt. It actually looked more like this: JESUSAVES. All the letters were blue except for those in the middle—USA—which were red. It was a telling icon of the confused syncretism of many Christians in America. Who saves? Jesus? The U.S.A.? Or, are the two so entwined that we can't tell the difference?[1]

Proverbs 29:18 (KJV) warns us that "where there is no vision, the people perish."[2] The story of the call of the prophet Samuel begins by lamenting the state of affairs in Israel under the corrupt leadership of Eli's wicked sons with the description, "The word of the Lord was rare in those days, visions were not widespread" (1 Samuel 3:1). It is all too evident, at the present time in the United States, that there is a serious famine of hearing the word of the Lord in our sanctuaries and therefore a corresponding lack of vision, symbolized in the narrative of 1 Samuel by Eli's dimness of sight (3:2). This is not, we might think as we enter the story, a good climate for the emergence of a "seer," a person of clear vision. But that would be to underestimate the surprising power of God, who raises up prophets and seers precisely when it seems least possible for them to emerge from whatever human resources happen to be around.

Just so, it is equally apparent in our own time, as in the narrative of 1 Samuel, that the lamp of the Lord, however low and flickering its flame, has not quite gone out (3:3). Indeed, this is precisely the liminal time when God characteristically acts with unexpected power and when unsuspecting sanctuary sleepers are suddenly called to become dreamers, visionaries, and prophets. It is not required of them that they desire to hear a word from the Lord or even that they recognize the voice of God at the beginning. In fact, quite the contrary: the biblical narrative of 1 Samuel 3 suggests that prophets have to be taught how to discern the word of the Lord before they can be expected to preach it with integrity and power. Like young Samuel, we preachers must learn first to pray, "Speak, Lord, for your servant is listening" (3:10, KJV), then to wait resolutely in the darkness that surrounds us and fills us, patient and expectant in the presence of the apparently opaque text. What we hear in that darkness may indeed make our own ears and the ears of all who hear it tingle (3:11).

---

1. Gunter, Matthew, "Taking Up The Cross In A Time of War," St. Barnabas Episcopal Church, Glen Ellyn, Illinois, Lent 2, Year B, 3/16/03.

2. All other biblical quotations are taken from the NRSV unless otherwise indicated.

Biblical prophets consistently materialize—sometimes seemingly out of thin air like Elijah in 1 Kings 17:1—when the leadership of the nation has forgotten God's covenant and has instead pursued its own nationalistic and materialistic interests, often at the expense of the people of Israel themselves. For this reason, properly speaking, the Elijah narrative begins with the summary description of King Ahab's rule in 1 Kings 16:29–30. which states matter of factly, "Ahab son of Omri did evil in the sight of the Lord more than all who were before him" (16:30).

The prophetic critique of the *selfish materialism* of the kings of Israel at the expense of the people is well demonstrated in the story of the prophet Elijah's opposition to King Ahab in the matter of his murder of Naboth and the seizure of his vineyard recounted in 1 Kings 21. Elsewhere in the ancient Near East, kings rode roughshod over the rights of their subjects, claiming to have absolute control over their bodies and their possessions. But in Israel, the king was never above the law and could be held accountable to divine judgment for wrongs done to fellow Israelites. Ancient legal tradition forbade the alienation of ancestral land, such as the vineyard of Naboth, which was located beside King Ahab's palace. The king desired it for his vegetable garden and offered to give Naboth comparable land elsewhere or money for it, but Naboth rightly responded, "I will not give you my ancestral inheritance" (21:4). So the king sulked and refused to eat until Queen Jezebel reassured him that he did indeed "govern Israel" and could take Naboth's vineyard with or without his consent. She arranged for false testimony that Naboth had cursed God and the king. She saw to his stoning as well. After this judicial murder was successfully carried out and Naboth lay dead, Ahab went to take possession of it (21:16).

The very next verse describes God's reaction. "Then the word of the Lord came to Elijah the Tishbite, saying: Go down to meet King Ahab of Israel. . . . You shall say to him, 'Thus says the Lord: Have you killed, and also taken possession?' " (21:17–19). The prophet predicts that dogs will lick up the blood of Ahab in the same place where they licked up the blood of Naboth and that the dogs will eat Jezebel within the bounds of Jezreel. Ahab's reaction is telling: "Have you found me, O my enemy?" to which Elijah replies, "I have found you. Because you have sold yourself to do what is evil in the sight of the Lord, I will bring disaster on you" (21:20). The sudden appearance of Elijah to pronounce judgment upon Ahab is God's direct response to the wrongful act of aggression committed by King Ahab and Queen Jezebel.

The prophetic critique of the *nationalistic militarism* of the kings of Israel at the expense of the people is clearly seen in the story of the prophet Michaiah ben Imlah's opposition to Ahab, King of Israel, and his vassal King Jehoshaphat of Judah (1 Kings 22). King Ahab and Ben-hadad of

Aram had a peace treaty that had lasted for three years, until King Ahab suddenly said one day, "Do you know that Ramoth-gilead belongs to us, yet we are doing nothing to take it out of the hand of the king of Aram?" (22:3) Ahab enlisted Jehoshaphat's aid against Ben-hadad, and the vassal king of Judah agreed but asked Ahab to "inquire first for the word of the Lord" (22:5). So Ahab gathered all his court prophets, about four hundred of them, and asked, "Shall I go to battle against Ramoth-gilead, or shall I refrain?" They told him exactly what he wanted to hear:[3] "Go up; for the Lord will give it into the hand of the king" (22:6).

Apparently King Jehoshaphat still had some doubts. "Is there no other prophet of the Lord here of whom we may inquire?" Ahab admitted that there was, of course, Michaiah ben Imlah, "but I hate him, for he never prophesies anything favorable about me, but only disaster" (22:8). Eventually Michaiah was brought to the king and, when pushed to tell the truth, he said of the coming battle: "I saw all Israel scattered on the mountains, like sheep that have no shepherd; and the Lord said, 'These have no master; let each one go home in peace'" (22:17). Michaiah's prediction of Israel's defeat and Ahab's death infuriated the king of Israel. He ordered Michaiah to be imprisoned and fed only bread and water "until I come in peace" (22:27). Michaiah replied, "If you return in peace, the Lord has not spoken by me" (22:28). The rest of the story is predictably tragic: the armies of Israel and Judah were massacred on the hillsides of Ramoth-gilead. Ahab disguised himself in battle but was killed anyway, his blood flowing into the bottom of his chariot. The Israelites remaining alive were scattered like sheep without a shepherd. The chariot of King Ahab was washed out by the pool of Samaria, where Naboth had been stoned. There the dogs licked up Ahab's blood as prophesied earlier by Elijah (22:38). We are not told whether Michaiah ben Imlah was released from prison or not.

What these stories (and many others like them) tell us is that whenever Israel's kings lose the vision of themselves as God's agents, and forget the word that requires them to serve the people committed to their charge, and begin to believe their own materialistic and militaristic propaganda, God responds by raising up a "seer" like Samuel or a prophet like Elijah or Michaiah ben Imlah—someone who first "sees" (from God's perspective) and then "speaks" for the Lord; someone who first "hears" (listens attentively) and then "proclaims" the word of the Lord. Over against the materialism and militarism of the kings of Israel, the prophet announces "the dream of God"[4] on behalf of Israel's true king, YHWH. Not surprisingly, this

---

3. The text implies that they are speaking in unison!

4. Dozier, Verna, *The Dream of God: A Call to Return* (Cambridge, Mass.: Cowley Press, 1991).

word of the Lord repeatedly takes the form of a "word spoken against" the royal propaganda and a "counter-vision" to the assurances of the court prophets who prophesy for hire. Such an antagonistic function is clearly secondary to the main purpose of "speaking for" (pro-phêtês) God's dream for the nation. Nevertheless, precisely at that point in the story, the prophet is routinely called "unpatriotic" by the royal power (1 Kings 21:20) and is not infrequently cast into prison (1 Kings 22:27).

If we needed any confirmation that the pattern described in the biblical narratives is distinctly relevant to the events of our own time and situation, we have only to review the recent confrontation between former President George H. W. Bush, who is an Episcopalian, and Frank Griswold, Presiding Bishop of the Episcopal Church in the United States of America. In January of the year 2003, Bishop Griswold sounded the same warning that many other Anglican church leaders around the world (including Archbishop of Canterbury Rowan Williams and Former Archbishop of Capetown Desmond Tutu) had also given. Many thought Griswold was merely stating the obvious when he said of the United States, "We are loathed, and I think the world has every right to loathe us, because they see us as greedy, self-interested and almost totally unconcerned about poverty, disease, and suffering."

In a speech given January 31, 2003, in Stamford, Connecticut, former President Bush called these comments "highly offensive" and (predictably) countered with the charge of unpatriotism: "We are the most generous, fairest nation in the world," said Bush. "How can this man of God think so little of the United States? . . . Unlike the bishop, I never feel the need to apologize for this great country." Undeterred by the clear implication that criticism of the nation's foreign policy is disloyalty to the nation itself, Bishop Griswold responded: "If we are a nation under God, . . . then we have to adopt God's perspectives, which means a superpower must be a super servant. . . . Religious leaders and people of faith need to be publicly and forcefully critical of America's foreign policy, particularly when the future of the world seems so precarious."[5]

The strategy of discounting the prophetic word as "unpatriotic" is so predictable in our nation that Martin Luther King, Jr. warned about it long ago:

In the days ahead, we must not consider it unpatriotic to raise certain questions about our national character. We must begin to ask, 'Why are there forty million poor people in a nation overflowing with such

---

5. "Fear grips America, Episcopal leader says," by Cathleen Falsani, Religion Reporter, *Chicago Sun Times*, February 17, 2003.

unbelievable affluence? Why has our nation placed itself in the position of being God's military agent on earth . . . ? Why have we substituted the arrogant undertaking of policing the whole world for the high task of putting our own house in order?"[6]

Presiding Bishop Griswold underlined the connection between true patriotism and God's compassion for the poor when he concluded:

The voices that are being raised up now are equivalent to the prophets of old saying, 'Wait a minute; what is justice here rather than retribution and revenge?' How are we called to be a people of mercy, a people of compassion, a people who see the world as God's world and that everyone in it is loved by God?[7]

It is hardly an accident that Frank Griswold, Desmond Tutu, Rowan Williams, Marian Wright Edelman, Martin Luther King, Jr., and others have found themselves proclaiming the dream of God in opposition to the fantasies of imperial America. Faithful Christian preaching is inherently prophetic because it seeks to bring "God's perspectives" to bear on the perceived realities of our lives and the lives of the members of our congregations.

But what does any of that have to do with the apostle Paul? In order to answer that question, it will be useful to review some homiletical assumptions about what faithfulness to the biblical text requires of the preacher.

2. "Be Imitators of Me, As I Am of Christ" (1 Corinthians 11:1)

Fred Craddock has counseled generations of preachers to follow the lead of the biblical text itself in our explication and interpretation of it.[8] If we listen carefully, the Bible will tell us how it wants to be preached. To become a servant of God's Word in this way of understanding requires learning to allow the content of the text to set the agenda for the sermon. But that is only the beginning: what is also required in our preaching is a disciplined and careful re-enactment of the movement of the text itself.

---

6. Martin Luther King, Jr., exact source of quotation unknown after extensive search, cited in part in Cone, James H., *Martin & Malcolm & America: A Dream or a Nightmare* (Maryknoll, New York: Orbis, 1991), 224.

7. "Fear grips America, Episcopal leader says," Cathleen Falsani, Religion Reporter, *Chicago Sun Times*, February 17, 2003.

8. Fred Craddock, *As One Without Authority: Essays on Inductive Preaching* (Nashville: Abingdon, 1971, 1974, 1979); *Overhearing the Gospel* (Nashville: Abingdon, 1978); *Preaching* (Nashville: Abingdon, 1985).

Faithful interpreters of the text will pay attention to its genre; trace the plot of its narrative; note carefully its rhetorical structure; linger over any of its cracks and fissures, fault lines, ambiguities, or idiosyncrasies; observe its special vocabulary; sense its mood; and finally attempt to let the sermon we preach, in its new setting, imitate what the biblical text says and does in its own setting.

To follow the movement of the biblical text is to walk behind it as its shadow and dancing partner: we move when it moves; we stop when it stops; though not, of course, mechanistically. There may come a time in the sermon when the text moves to the right and the preacher moves to the left, whether for dramatic effect—like one of those old Groucho-Marx-in-a-nightshirt-and-the-man-in-the-mirror comedy routines—or, more seriously, because to say *exactly* what the text says would not at all be to say either precisely what the text said then or what the text is actually saying now. The integrity of the dance is preserved both in the *mimesis* and in the well-considered innovation; in either response, the sermon is truly a "reflection" of the biblical text.

What would it be like to undertake a homiletical discipline in which the preacher follows not only the lead of the biblical text but also the lead of its author? This would be comparable to studying not only the technique, the brush strokes, of a great painter, but seeking also to understand his theory of painting, his reason for living, and his view of reality as a whole. Not only would we learn how to copy the meter and the rhyme scheme of a skilled poet; we would also imitate her choice of subjects, internalize her politics, adopt her puritanical lifestyle. In order to do that, we would need to undertake an extensive socio-historical investigation of our subject to get the details right.[9] Does this learning-by-imitating model make sense when we consider the authors of Scripture? We commonly speak of the Gospels as portraits of Jesus. We celebrate the poetry of Revelation and the rhetorical beauty of Hebrews. How well would it work for preachers to apprentice ourselves to the biblical writers whose texts we wanted to "reflect" in our preaching? Could we work with their tools to learn their trade? Could we try on their clothes to see about the fit?

If this sounds like an intriguing possibility, we are immediately confronted with the reality that in most cases we don't know enough about the authors of the biblical texts for this hypothetical question to be taken seriously. All the information we have about the four evangelists is the tradition of the

---

9. Even then, it might finally prove difficult to live in the role of someone whose work we admire greatly but whose character or vocation seems strangely disconcerting. We might appreciate and learn to imitate the style of van Gogh's paintings and Poe's short stories without wanting to become quite like them personally.

names that may or may not actually have belonged to them. We have no idea who "Mark" was or where "Luke" lived. We have their writings—about 37,800 words in the case of the writer of Luke-Acts—but we know next to nothing about their lives, their personalities, their struggles or successes, or their church communities. The opposite pattern is true in the case of Jesus of Nazareth himself, the subject of the Gospels—about whom we know a reasonable amount historically and can make intelligent guesses about even more, even though we have none of his writings.

There is, however, at least one New Testament author for whom we have both fairly reliable historical information and substantial literary remains. The apostle Paul is unmatched among followers of Jesus in terms of the writings produced by him and about him: his letters were already considered "Scripture" by the end of the first century and his reputation was so strong that he had become a serious problem, both for those who agreed with him and those who opposed him. It is not an overstatement to say that Paul dominates the writings of the New Testament: thirteen of its twenty-seven books are attributed to him by name; an additional book was admitted to the canon because he was believed to have written it; several others were clearly influenced by him; another spends more than half its pages describing his career as a missionary; even some parts of the Gospels seem to be in debate or at least in conversation with Paul. Long after his death, Paul continued to influence the imagination of the early Christian world. Outside of the canon are found several apocryphal acts of Paul, including the controversial Acts of Paul and Thecla, yet another letter to the Corinthians, the (now-missing) letter to the Laodiceans, and a lengthy apocryphal correspondence between Paul and the Stoic philosopher Seneca.

More importantly for those of us who would like to learn how to preach Paul's letters by studying Paul the person, we have a substantial body of Paul's correspondence in which his strong personality is clearly revealed. On the one hand, it is clear that in the seven uncontested letters of Paul (Romans, 1 and 2 Corinthians, Galatians, Philippians, 1 Thessalonians, and Philemon), we have an opportunity to watch an artist at work in a variety of settings and under significantly different conditions. On the other hand, because the genre of a letter is so revealing of its author, we can see at least something of the interaction between the texts he wrote and the person he was. We scarcely know the Lukan author from whom we have considerably more words, but Paul's personality is sharply defined through his work. His letters are the most autobiographical of the early Christian canonical writings.

What Jeremiah is to the Old Testament in terms of candid self-revelation, Paul is to the New Testament. This gospel-driven apostle writes with passion and conviction. We hear his tenderness and affection in 1 Thessalonians and Philippians; we see his blazing anger in Galatians and Second Corinthians; we feel the pathos of his concern for Israel in Romans 9–11. Paul was a preacher of considerable eloquence, although he claims not to be gifted in rhetoric. Like the majority of preachers today, Paul was first of all a pastor. He often speaks of his ongoing concern for the struggling churches he had planted and grown. What would it be like to learn how to imitate the movement of the Pauline biblical texts by following Paul around for awhile, learning his steps, making his moves? [10] This question becomes fascinating when we consider that Paul deliberately summoned his first hearers to imitate him as he strove to imitate Christ: "I appeal to you then, be imitators of me" (1 Corinthians 4:16).

Suppose we took Paul up on his invitation? What could we learn? I suggest that we might learn at least the following: first, that the usual dichotomy between "pastoral" and "prophetic" styles of ministry should be abandoned as a false alternative; second, that to be "prophetic" is to be inherently *conservative* (in the sense of standing within a received and honored tradition) and inevitably *radical* (in the sense of going to the root causes of issues); third, that pastoring prophetically implies living imaginatively in the midst of community; the "seer" sees not a way out of the church but a way into a deeper understanding of what the church is; finally, that preaching as a prophet-pastor is fraught with spiritual dangers and temptations. Among the several spiritual disciplines that might be adopted by prophet pastors who preach, the most important, I shall conclude, is remaining focused on Jesus Christ and on following him in the way of the cross.

3. Is Saul Also Among the Prophets? Discarding the Pastor or Prophet Alternative

The first result of studying in Paul's preaching workshop is surely that the usual dichotomy between "pastoral" and "prophetic" styles of ministry must be recognized as a false alternative and abandoned as quickly as possible. Similar false dichotomies (between prophetic and priestly, cultic and apocalyptic) were once prevalent in biblical higher criticism until the discovery of the Dead Sea Scrolls in the mid-twentieth century, where a reforming remnant monastic desert community either produced

---

10. I note here two recent books whose titles suggest that this is indeed our task: James W. Thompson's *Preaching Like Paul: Homiletical Wisdom for Today* (Louisville: Westminster John Knox, 2001) and Nancy Lammers Gross's *If You Cannot Preach Like Paul* (Grand Rapids: Eerdmans, 2002). The present project is to be distinguished from both of these, while recognizing their useful contributions to the discussion.

or preserved scrolls connected to the priestly figure of Melchizedek and the Temple and apocalyptic holy warfare against the sons of darkness. Categories imposed from the assumptions prevalent in our own time were shown to be distinctly irrelevant for understanding forms of Second Temple Judaism.

That recent historical experience is then useful for our own self-understanding: do these either/or categories work even in our own culture? What is a prophet? What is a pastor? Does the usual dichotomy "work" only when the terms are defined in a particular way that minimizes what they have in common in order to highlight their differences and make possible the contrast that is pre-assumed? Then we should not be surprised when the term "pastoral" is reduced to non-confrontational caregiving designed to maintain the status quo ante church, or the term "prophetic" is reserved for those "lone rangers" who cannot get along in Christian community because they are "unrealistic" and uncompromising. Perhaps our "imitation of Paul," who saw himself as a prophet and who pastored early Christian communities, can lead us to a more sophisticated and dialectical understanding of the pastoral and the prophetic aspects of Christian community.[11]

Paul, perhaps very much like Jesus before him, seems to have seen himself in the tradition of Israel's prophets, especially Jeremiah and Isaiah. Paul describes his apostolic vocation at the beginning of Galatians with language that seems designed to evoke Jeremiah's call story. When Paul refers to the time when God "who had set me apart before I was born and called me through his grace" was pleased to reveal God's Son in or through Paul (Galatians 1:15), his language recalls Jeremiah 1:4–5:

Now the word of the Lord came to me saying,
"Before I formed you in the womb I knew you,
and before you were born I consecrated you;
I appointed you a prophet to the nations."[12]

---

11. I have been greatly helped in my thinking about this subject by two books. The first, *The Pastor as Prophet* (edited by Earl E. Shelp and Ronald H. Sunderland, New York: Pilgrim Press, 1985), is a collection of essays by Stanley Hauerwas, Walter Brueggemann, John Howard Yoder, George MacRae, Daniel L. Migliore, and Jorge Lara-Braud. The second is Douglas Harink's exciting new book, *Paul Among the Postliberals: Pauline Theology Beyond Christendom and Modernity* (Grand Rapids: Brazos Press, 2003).

12. See also Romans 11:13, where Paul describes himself as an apostle to the Gentiles, that is, one sent with a commission to proclaim the Gospel to the nations.

and also Isaiah 49:1–6:

> Listen to me, O coastlands,
> Pay attention, you peoples from far away!
> The Lord called me before I was born,
> While I was in my mother's womb he named me.

> . . . He says, "It is too light a thing that you should be my servant
> To raise up the tribes of Jacob
> And to restore the survivors of Israel;
> I will give you as a light to the nations,
> That my salvation may reach to the end of the earth."

Paul's self-identification with Jeremiah and Isaiah is not limited to the prophetic call narrative. In Romans 10:15–16, Paul describes his work of preaching the Gospel using the language of Isaiah 52:7, "How beautiful are the feet of those who bring good news!" At the same time, he also understands the rejection of his Gospel in the same framework of Isaiah's proclamation of God's good news and its rejection by the people of Israel, drawing the quotation this time from Isaiah 53:1, "Who has believed our message?" Paul claims such a prophetic role only indirectly,[13] but his apostleship rests on the vision of the risen Lord in which he was called and commissioned (Galatians 1:1 and 1:11–12, 1 Corinthians 9:1, 15:8–9) to preach the Gospel (1 Corinthians 1:17).

We get some clues as to the importance of prophecy for Paul by studying 1 Corinthians 14. Already in 1 Corinthians 12:10 and 28, Paul had listed prophecy or prophets among the specialized gifts of the Holy Spirit within the body of Christ. In chapter 14, however, he contrasts the gifts of speaking in tongues, which the Corinthians seem to have valued highly, and of prophecy, which Paul himself prefers. The gift of prophecy, says Paul, serves to build up the entire community while the gift of tongues only builds up the individual to whom it is given. For Paul, prophecy and pastoral care are inextricably linked; he sees himself both as pastor to the community and as one delivering prophecy to the assembly (14:6 and 19).[14] The purpose of prophecy is the upbuilding and encouragement of the church.[15]

---

13. George W. MacRae, "Paul, Prophet and Spiritual Leader," in *The Pastor as Prophet* (eds. Shelp and Sunderland, New York: Pilgrim, 1985), 99.

14. Even if these verses use the first person as exemplary rhetoric, which seems likely, Paul has twice urged the Corinthians specifically to imitate him, as he imitates Christ (4:16 and 11:1). The first-person rhetorical example, whether it refers to Paul personally or not, is part of the same pattern.

15. MacRae, op. cit., 109.

4. "I deliver to you what I also received . . .": The Prophet-Pastor as Radical Conservative

If we continue to study the art of preaching with Paul, working beside him as apprentices in his studio, we will quickly discover a second important and perhaps unanticipated phenomenon: the inherent conservatism of the prophetic vocation. To be prophetic is to be profoundly conservative in the classic sense of standing within a received and honored tradition to which one is unswervingly loyal. The biblical prophets kept calling the people of Israel back to the covenant obligations, which they were tempted to ignore, back to the One God whom they were tempted to abandon for some idol or another, back to the only real source of power and hope when they were tempted to form military alliances with political powers they could see and hear. In the same way, it is because the prophets care intensely about the moral shape of society that they assault every social disorder.[16] Walter Brueggemann describes the prophetic construal of social and political reality as having the following features: society consists in an organization of social power; it is derived from and dependent upon the management, control, and articulation of social symbols; the organization of social power and the administration of social symbols are linked in a social system that defines and legitimates all of life. Therefore, "the system is the solution" in the sense that the social organization of power and symbols is an absolute given. The only alternative to the social system is chaos, so the prophet's energies go into reformation of the present social system, not its abolition.[17]

The inherent conservatism of Paul's social and political worldview is signaled, among other things, by his understanding of tradition and the role of the Scriptures in his pastoral theology. At 1 Corinthians 11:23, "For I received from the Lord what I also handed on to you, that the Lord Jesus on the night when he was betrayed took a loaf of bread . . . ," Paul frames his teaching about the Lord's Supper in the context of the communal memory of the last supper of Jesus with his disciples. That communal memory serves as the plumbline by which to measure the deviant social practices in the Eucharist at Corinth that he is writing to reform. At 1 Corinthians 15:3, Paul again uses the standard terms for receiving and handing on a fixed body of tradition as he speaks of the resurrection: "For I handed on to you as of first importance what I in turn had received: that Christ died for our sins in accordance with the scriptures, and that he was buried, and that he was raised on the third day in accordance with the

---

16. Brueggemann, Walter, "The Prophet as a Destabilizing Presence," in *The Pastor as Prophet*, 49.

17. Brueggemann, Walter, op. cit., 50–51.

scriptures. . . ." Once again, the communal memory of the death and resurrection of the Lord Jesus "in accordance with the scriptures" forms the ground upon which Paul can stand to appeal to the Corinthians to take the reality of the Resurrection seriously in reforming their life together. Paul's letters are laced with such references to tradition in the form of hymnic and credal fragments, though not usually as clearly identified as the two examples above, that would have served as warrants for his theological and ethical arguments.

Paul's phrase, "according to the scriptures," points to a second aspect of his profoundly conservative worldview. It is the same God who made the covenant promises to Israel who also raised Christ Jesus from the dead and has called into being "the Israel of God" (Galatians 6:16) that is composed of Jewish and Gentile Christians praising God together in one body. Time and time again, Paul revisits Israel's sacred Scriptures, "the oracles of God" (Romans 3:2), in order to understand the present mysterious action of Israel's God. Because God is faithful and reliable, the One who makes promises and keeps them, God's word spoken so long ago in the Scriptures holds the key for the understanding of the end times in which Paul and his churches are presently living. Paul understands these Scriptures to speak directly to the situation of himself and his congregations, even to the point of prescribing the actions the community should take against troublemakers within it (Galatians 4:30, 1 Corinthians 5:13). For Paul, "the system is the solution" in the profoundest sense of the term: he cannot imagine any reality outside of the God who made covenant promises to Israel's ancestors about the inclusion of the Gentiles within the traditional holy writings of Israel.[18]

Ernst Käsemann helpfully identified a particular role of early Christian prophets: to formulate sayings of the Lord, which were attributed to Jesus in accounts of his life and teaching, applicable to the new situations and crises in which the church found itself after the Resurrection. Käsemann called them "sentences of holy law." While the particulars of his theory have largely been discarded by subsequent scholars, the basic outline remains useful, for early Christian prophets in general and for Paul in particular.[19] In Paul's case, we see him working back and forth between traditional sayings of the Lord, which have clearly already assumed an importance not unlike that of Scripture for the community (that is, they

---

18. This in no way denies that Paul lived fully into the hellenistic assumptions of the Graeco-Roman worldview in which he and everyone else in his time found themselves. These cultural assumptions were factored into a reality already defined by the world depicted in Israel's scriptures and the interpretive tradition that had grown up around them.

19. George W. MacRae, op. cit., 109.

too have an oracular function; they are expected to speak directly to the present situation), and his own judgment calls in the power of the Spirit of the same risen Lord. Thus Paul makes pronouncements on matters such as divorce and remarriage (1 Corinthians 7:10, 12, 25) and compensation of apostles (1 Corinthians 9:14) in conversation both with "sentences of holy law" and the Spirit behind them, not in slavish adherence to the letter of the saying, but in conformity with the pattern of the Messiah as seen in his death and Resurrection. In other words, Paul's theological and ethical innovations are generated in the most conservative way possible: they are securely anchored to traditions about Jesus and corrected by the power of the Spirit of Jesus speaking through an apostle who has been directly commissioned by the risen Lord to do this work.

At the same time to be prophetic is inevitably, as Brueggemann's title suggests, to be "a destabilizing presence" in the inherently conservative social world of the Scriptures and their interpretation by the community. The prophet in Israel is inevitably "radical," in the sense of going to the root causes of issues to expose their deformity and need of correction. The prophet is necessarily a "destabilizing presence" within the culture because the God of Israel, while reliable, trustworthy, and true, is not predictable and subject to the reductionist or trivializing formulations with which the false prophets (often court prophets for hire, in the service of the present rulers of the age) deal for their own purposes.

Paul's own world seems to have been thoroughly shaken by his encounter with the risen Lord. He describes himself in Philippians 3 as someone who had everything lined up correctly; his life was a puzzle in which all of the pieces fit perfectly; there was no need to question the synthesis that warranted his zealous persecution of the new messianic sect that read the Scriptures so differently from his own correct (orthodox) perspective. Some of my students were shocked when I commented that I had no difficulty visualizing Paul—before his "destabilization" by the risen Christ—flying a plane into the World Trade Center with no scruples about whether such an action could be done to the glory of God. Those uncircumcised pseudo-Jews who refused to keep God's commandments were sinners whom God would surely destroy, one way or another. Paul was only an agent of the powerful righteousness of God.

But when the righteousness of God was seen to have been broken in pain and humiliation on a Roman cross, the pagan instrument of torture for enemies of the empire, the form of political execution that was considered too vile and common for literary treatment but could only be the subject of vulgar and tasteless jokes, then the-world-as-Paul-knew-it collapsed into pieces and none of them fit anywhere for a while. Whatever actually happened in the mysterious and mind-changing encounter with Jesus Christ about which Paul is so reticent, he describes it on the one hand as an "apocalypse" (a revelation of Jesus Christ, cf. Galatians 1:12) and on the other hand as the total destruction of everything he thought he understood. "May I never boast of anything except the cross of our Lord Jesus Christ, by which the world has been crucified to me, and I to the world" (Galatians 6:14). Paul's world was invaded and destroyed by God's gracious action in Christ. It became the focus of his life and the subject of all his preaching, "for I decided to know nothing among you except Jesus Christ and him crucified" (1 Corinthians 2:2). Paul spoke of God's "new creation" in which neither circumcision nor uncircumcision mattered at all; what counted was faith working through love (Galatians 5:6, 6:15). God's new creation relativized the old age that was passing away; it called into question all the old interpretations of Scripture. Everything had to be re-thought in the light of the crucified and risen Lord whom Paul had persecuted but whom God had vindicated. Paul himself became a "destabilizer" of the tradition he had worked so zealously to defend.

As Paul Harink has put it succinctly,

the theme of the imitation of Christ or participation in Christ is . . . not about mystical, existential, or pietistic communion with Christ; it is rather a thoroughly *apocalyptic* theme. It is about participating with Christ in a conflict with the structures and powers of 'the present evil age' in the manner pioneered by Jesus in his life, trial, and crucifixion.[20]

5. Discerning the Body: The Prophet-Pastor's Loneliness Within Community

Still another result of apprenticing ourselves to the prophet-pastor Paul and learning to live into the new creation he describes so vividly in his letters is a changed conception of the prophet's role in the community. It has been traditional to describe the paradigmatic prophet of Israel as a lone wolf, isolated from the community in order to stand against it. That model of prophetic engagement is well illustrated by Elijah's complaint to God during the time of his persecution by Jezebel, after the great slaughter of the prophets of Baal at Mount Carmel. Jezebel had vowed revenge against Elijah, and everyone connected with him had gone into hiding. Elijah responded to the question about what he was doing in a cave in Mount Horeb with the following words:

---

20. Douglas Harink, *Paul Among the Postliberals: Pauline Theology Beyond Christendom and Modernity* (Grand Rapids: Brazos, 2003), 110.

I have been very zealous for the Lord, the God of hosts; for the Israelites have forsaken your covenant, thrown down your altars, and killed your prophets with the sword. I alone am left, and they are seeking my life to take it away (1 Kings 19:14).

We have already seen that Paul has reason to identify with Elijah in terms of his own zeal for the destruction of God's enemies before his encounter with the crucified and risen Christ. Does he also identify with Elijah as a lone wolf apostle, set over against the community? He does stand alone at Antioch, as he describes the confrontation with Peter and even Barnabas, over the issue of table *koinonia* between Jewish Christians and Gentile Christians after the challenge of the representatives from James (Galatians 2:11–14). But in Romans 11, Paul quotes the words of Elijah at Horeb above only to show how God refutes them. Employing an unusual word that construes God's reply to Elijah as an oracle applicable to Paul's own circumstances, he stresses the illusory nature of Elijah's perception that he is alone and isolated. The divine reply to Elijah is: "I have kept for myself seven thousand who have not bowed the knee to Baal" (Romans 11:4, 1 Kings 19:18).

It may be that part of the crucifixion of Paul's world involved the destruction of the illusion of the Phinehas-type zealot who acts alone, seeking to embody in his own person the saving righteous remnant of Israel. Instead, Paul may have had to learn that the way of the cross is the way of community, that pastoring prophetically implies living imaginatively in the midst of community. What the "seer" sees is not a way out of the church, but a way into a deeper understanding of what the church is and means.

That the prophet is not a lone wolf, but intimately invested and inevitably implicated in the life of the community of God's people is clear in the call story of Isaiah, dated to the year that King Uzziah died. Scholars have speculated that this might have been a vision of God that took its start from the fifteen-foot-high throne of God in the inner sanctuary of the temple in Jerusalem where Isaiah served as a priest. Since only the *hem* of God's robe filled the temple, the vision must have been of terrifying proportions. The prophet-priest's reaction is despair: "Woe is me! I am lost. [I am silenced,] for I am a man of unclean lips, I live among a people of unclean lips; yet my eyes have seen the King, the Lord of hosts!" (Isaiah 6:5). Isaiah knew apparently intuitively what Paul would have to struggle to learn and then to articulate again and again throughout his career, that the prophetic gift is given for the building up of the body as a whole, not for use in isolation from the community. Nowhere is this more important than when the prophet-pastor hears and subsequently speaks God's judgment on the community. As Reinhold Niebuhr once commented, "The prophet himself stands under the judgment which he preaches. If he does not know that, he is a false prophet."[21]

Paul's radical understanding of the body of Christ and the non-negotiable interconnectedness of its parts—precisely at the moment when some of them are saying, "We don't need you," and others are saying, "I'm not part of this"—has implications far beyond the prophet's own relationship to the rest of the body. It speaks directly to the danger associated with holiness that Isaiah described in his vision. Paul is horrified that some members of Corinth apparently see no connection between their "personal, private expressions of sexuality" and the holiness of the community as a body.

> Do you not know that your bodies are members of Christ? Should I therefore take the members of Christ and make them members of a prostitute? Never! Do you not know that whoever is united to a prostitute becomes one body with her? For it is said, "The two shall be one flesh." But anyone united to the Lord becomes one spirit with him (1 Corinthians 6:15–17).

Paul's point is that the persons engaged in sexual immorality sin not only against their own bodies but against the whole body of Christ, since each body is a sanctuary of the Holy Spirit that is sanctifying the entire body at once. God's holiness is dangerous and uncompromising. Because prophet and people are implicated together, both in sin and in God's judgment upon sin, the word "pastoral" cannot be used to justify a system of mutual failure to hold one another accountable to the high standards of God's holiness that must characterize the body of Christ. Nowhere is this clearer than in the sacrament that celebrates that unity, the Holy Eucharist.

Bishop William Wiedrich of the Diocese of Chicago used to tell the story of a parish where he had once served as rector that had difficulties with static electricity. The installation of new carpet in the sanctuary made the situation even more serious. Dry air and the new carpet combined to build up a substantial electrical charge. On the first Sunday after the new carpet was installed, Father Wiedrich celebrated the Eucharist. As he prepared to distribute the body of Christ, it happened that the first person at the altar rail was his senior warden, kneeling reverently with his mouth open to receive the sacrament. Father Wiedrich walked over to him and said the familiar words: "The Body of Christ, the Bread of Heaven." But as he

---

21. Reinhold Niebuhr, "The Test of True Prophecy" in *Beyond Tragedy: Essays on the Christian Interpretation of History* (New York: Charles Scribner's Sons, 1937, 1965), 110.

placed the wafer on the man's tongue, there was such a powerful electrical discharge that it knocked the warden on his back. The static electricity became such a problem that Wiedrich enlisted an acolyte to stand next to him so that he could touch the acolyte to take the shock rather than the people at the rail. The acolytes, in turn, began to draw straws to see which of them would have to serve as the rector's human grounding that morning. At least in that parish, people began to understand that celebrating the Lord's Supper is serious business and not altogether safe.[22]

This story illustrates in a light-hearted way something of what Paul may have meant when he stated, "Many of you are weak and ill, and some have died" (1 Corinthians 11:30) because of failure to discern the body of Christ. Paul's difficult words remind us that a body of Christ that practices the economic discrimination against the poorer members of the body that characterized Corinth will be judged as harshly as the body that tolerates sexual immorality among its members or the body that refuses to deal with its racism.

Peter Storey preached a sermon in the context of South African apartheid on Paul's comment about the social significance of the Eucharist, "For as often as you eat this bread and drink the cup, you proclaim the Lord's death until he comes" (1 Corinthians 11:26), as follows:

> The apostle tells us that every time we eat of this bread and drink of this cup, we are announcing the death of Jesus again. We must do this until he comes . . . There, concretely and visibly, in human history, the Son of God offered himself up for us all. It is done! But we are here today also because Calvary is *never* done. In another sense, so long as the sin and hurt and violence and hate of humankind continue, so long is Jesus nailed to that cross. And we need to cry out! We need to proclaim with tears that *the death of the Lord is happening again, right here around us.*[23]

It should be said clearly that the preaching of the cross can itself be a form of death. Preachers who name social sin out loud in the midst of a community that is determined not to see it should not expect a standing ovation, even if the preachers are careful to include themselves in the judgment of God they fear for their people. Therefore, in the midst of community, the work of the prophet is lonely. If the false prophets of the

---

22. Adapted from Matthew Gunter's sermon, "Discerning The Body," preached at the Virginia Seminary Chapel, March 12, 2002.

23. Peter Storey, *With God in the Crucible: Preaching Costly Discipleship* (Nashville, Abingdon, 2002), 134–35, emphasis original.

culture tell the people what they want to hear, then the prophet is often speaking the opposite of whatever the people are expecting to hear. Because they have been coached to expect reality in the particular form that the false prophets have packaged it, the prophet's long-range vision seems out of step at best.

Indeed, how could it be otherwise? The prophet speaks of God's dream in the context of the present nightmare. But the present illusion often seems much more attractive than the divine reality that the prophet proclaims. The prophet, speaking from the perspective of God's inbreaking future, shouts "Fallen is Babylon!" but Babylon at present stands tall, with glorious towers and whitewashed walls. The prophet-pastor invites discernment: Which world is the real world? Where is God's activity to be discovered in the present? What is reality and what is illusion? Where is slavery and where is freedom? What issues are trivial and which are matters of life and death?

That Moses was the quintessential prophet-pastor of Israel reminds us that behind every prophet and every prophetic call is the story of the Exodus from slavery and death in Egypt, which had its safe, predictable, and familiar features, compared to life in the wilderness with God's holiness. Quaker activist Ched Myers speaks of "livin' along de Nile" (a long denial) of the reality of the costs of slavery as a form of contemporary political and economic addiction. Just as the drug addict will do everything possible not to see the reality of the certain death that results from shooting up (bondage to Pharaoh) in order to avoid the scarey and undefined threat of the wilderness experience of recovery, so it is with our culture as a whole. We have a vested interest in not seeing anything that would require us to change. "We're fine," says the miner. "The canary's just taking a nap." We're fine—insert appropriate rationalization for addiction or prevailing national mythology in support of materialism and militarism here—so we don't need to change. "The mark of false prophecy," according to Reinhold Niebuhr, "is that it assures the sinner peace and security within the terms of his [or her] sinful ambitions."[24]

What then is a prophet? Is a prophet the one who sees the same thing everyone else sees only the prophet is not in denial? Or are prophets forced by God—often against their own wills—to awaken to a truth from which there is no going back to sleep? Are prophets doomed to live out of the nightmare that has awakened them, when everyone else is peacefully enjoying the American dream? As Paul says of slavery to sin, "The end of those things is death" (Romans 6:21).

---

24. Reinhold Niebuhr, op. cit., 94.

Conclusion: Eyes on the Prize: Spiritual Dangers of the Prophet-Pastor-Preacher

Because the message of the prophet-pastor is both inherently conservative and radically innovative and because the prophet-pastor often experiences the loneliness that results from sustained commitment to accountability within community, there are special temptations that assault the preacher attempting to live out this vocation. Those who wish to imitate not only the homiletical moves in Paul's letters but also the prophet-pastor himself as he prepares to write and preach them will be particularly interested in the disciplines he adopts for himself and urges upon the members of the congregations entrusted to his care. For Paul, the athletic metaphors he uses (getting his body in training, running the race, competing for the prize) were as much about the disciplined life of the visionary leader as they were about the life of the church.

In this last section of my essay, I am helped considerably by a contemporary preacher who has reflected deeply on the spiritual dangers of prophetic preaching while pastoring a congregation. Mariann Edgar Budde writes:

> The prophetic task is fraught with peril, from without and from within, and we who are called to leadership of any kind in Christ's church need to have our wits about us as we contemplate this particular dimension of our vocation. The first thing to say about it is that it is non-negotiable.[25]

Budde quotes Brueggemann on the "peculiar institutional provision" of the people of Israel, which is prophecy. Prophetic speech, he says, is "not an accident, not an intrusion, not an extra in the life of the community," but intrinsic to it, "assuring that God's people would be held accountable to the transcendent purpose of God."[26] Prophets are to be accorded the highest honor.

Except, of course, in their own country, and among their own people, and within their own congregations. The external peril to the prophetic tradition is well known: the prophet who can somehow be discounted or relativized is ignored; the prophet who can be intimidated or removed is silenced; the prophet who can be neither ignored nor silenced is killed. Below the balcony of the Lorraine Motel in Memphis, where Martin

---

25. Mariann Edgar Budde, Sermon for 4 Pentecost, Year B, preached at Virginia Theological Seminary Chapel, February 5, 2003.

26. Walter Brueggemann, *A Lectionary Commentary on the NRSV—Year B* (Westminster Press, 1993), 126.

Luther King, Jr., was shot at the age of thirty-nine, there is a plaque with the words of Joseph's brothers in Genesis 37:19–20, according to the King James Version, "They said one to another, Behold this dreamer cometh . . . Let us slay him . . . and we shall see what will become of his dreams." Ironically, in the decades since his death, King has been remembered primarily as the spellbinding orator who delivered the "I Have a Dream" speech at the Lincoln Monument. "Boulevards, community centers, parks, buildings, and monuments have been named in his honor . . . The Dreamer is honored; why he was killed is glossed over. The burning prophetic fire in him that illumined the dark recesses of our national life—what he called the triple evils of racism, materialism, and militarism—is still too intense for our timid hearts."[27]

What about the internal perils of prophecy? If there is resistance to the prophetic message and denial within the listeners, what about resistance and denial within the prophetic preacher? In Deuteronomy 18:20, the Lord warns Israel's greatest prophet Moses of the two most dangerous spiritual temptations for prophets: speaking in the name of other gods and presuming to speak in God's name a word that God has not commanded the prophet to speak. The prophet who does these things is threatened with death.

"Saying in the name of other gods," Budde says, is a biblical way of naming that which, while it may be *proffered* as prophetic speech, is *actually* nothing more than "saying what others want to hear, or what we ourselves wish were true." In the sermon on Jeremiah 28:5–9, which appears elsewhere in the present volume, she describes Jeremiah's confrontation with Hananiah, his contemporary at the time of the Babylonian invasion.

Hananiah, a prophet of the king, presumably speaking for God, assures the nation that the Babylonian occupation will be short. There is no need to worry, no need to make dramatic adjustments. God will provide. Peace and prosperity will return shortly. Jeremiah is stunned by Hananiah's words, for it is the opposite of what he himself has heard from God—that the occupation and exile will be long and that the people must learn the spiritual lessons of hardship.[28]

Hananiah's "prophecy" illustrates the illusion that the children of God will be accorded some special protection from the results of their sin, that

---

27. Richard Deats, *Martin Luther King, Jr., Spirit-Led Prophet* (New York: New City Press, 2000), 15.

28. Mariann Edgar Budde, "Welcoming Prophets—Receiving Their Rewards," in this volume, 61.

God will somehow fix it so that the natural forces of cause and effect will be suspended and the people won't have to face the consequences of their own actions. If Hananiah was not simply lying in order to tell the people what he thought would reassure them, then he spoke out of the same combination of blindness and wishful thinking that characterized the nation's leaders. He was in denial not only about the seriousness of the political situation but also about the reality of God's judgment. Speaking in the name of the gods of "peace and prosperity" and "security from terror," Hananiah spoke words that were easy to hear and easier to believe; they fed into the national delusion. Jeremiah's words were hard to hear; believing them would require becoming sober, awakening from the dream of denial, and facing the nightmare of God's judgment upon sin. No wonder the people chose to hear Hananiah instead. But, as Budde comments above, "As it turned out, Jeremiah was right and Hananiah was wrong, which is one reason Jeremiah got his book in the Bible and Hananiah didn't."[29]

Budde calls the second internal peril, presuming to speak a word that God has not commanded, "simply arrogance, the tyranny of being right."

"From the place we are right," writes the poet Yehuda Amichai, "flowers will never grow in the spring. The place where we are right is hard and trampled like a yard." We do God no service by speaking from self-righteous certainty. For from the place we are right, we lose sight of love. Most biblical prophets took no pleasure in their words of judgment. More important, they stood with their people under that judgment out of love and in hope for a better day. If we speak without love, no matter the truth of our words, we do not speak for God.[30]

Paul would agree completely. "If I have prophetic powers, and understand all mysteries and all knowledge, and if I have all faith, so as to remove mountains, but do not have love, I am nothing" (1 Corinthians 13:2). One of the most important spiritual disciplines for prophetic preachers is that of self-examination in preparation for confession. We could do worse than focus on the three Christian virtues that Paul privileges in 1 Corinthians 13. Do we have the kind of faith, whether it removes mountains or not, that allows us to hear and therefore to preach that nothing in all creation will be able to separate us from the love of God in Christ Jesus our Lord? (Romans 8:39). Have we hoped in Christ for this life only, so that we are of all people most to be pitied? Or is our hope based in the promise of God that "as all die in Adam, so all will be made alive in

---

29. Budde, ibid.
30. Budde, "Sermon for 4 Pentecost, Year B" cited earlier.

Christ?" (1 Corinthians 15:22). Are we willing to subject our prophetic preaching to a standard of love which is patient, kind, not envious, boastful, arrogant or rude, does not insist on its own way, is not irritable or resentful, does not rejoice in wrongdoing but in the truth, and which bears, believes, hopes, endures all things? (1 Corinthians 13:4–7). Only then are we preaching in imitation of Paul, in imitation of Christ.

Reinhold Niebuhr ends his remarks on the difference between true and false prophecy with these words:

> It is instructive that the same Jeremiah who spoke so uncompromisingly against the false prophets tried to return his prophetic commission to God. He was not certain that he was worthy of it, and he doubted his courage to maintain the integrity of the word of God against the resistance of a whole generation which demanded security from religion and rejected the prophet who could offer no security on this side of repentance.[31]

So Martin Luther King, Jr. was described by friends who knew him well as a man who was deeply troubled that so many others had done as much or more than he had and they had gained no recognition from it. He felt that he had not earned and did not deserve the acclaim he was receiving.[32] But unlike others, he also saw himself as one captive to the word of God and constrained by God to preach an unpopular word.

> Before I was a civil rights leader, I answered a call, and when God speaks, who can but prophesy? I answered a call which left the Spirit of the Lord upon me and anointed me to preach the gospel. . . . I decided then that I was going to tell the truth as God revealed it to me. No matter how many people disagreed with me, I decided that I was going to tell the truth.[33]

King knew that the roles of pastor, prophet, and preacher are inseparable because the call to preaching is the call to speak the truth of God as it is revealed in prayer, study, and concern for the people of God, regardless of who is affected by its judgment or the personal costs to the

---

31. Reinhold Niebuhr, op. cit., 110.

32. David J. Garrow, *Bearing the Cross: Martin Luther King, Jr., and the Southern Christian Leadership Conference* (New York: Vintage Books, 1986), 588.

33. King, "Why I Am Opposed to the War in Vietnam," address given April 30, 1967, at Ebenezer Baptist Church, Atlanta, cited in Cone, op. cit., 240.

preacher. He seems to have identified with both Jeremiah and Paul when he said:

> You called me to Ebenezer, and you may turn me out of here. But you can't turn me out of the ministry, because I got . . . my appointment from God Almighty, and anything I want to say I'm going to say it from this pulpit. It may hurt somebody. I don't know about that. Somebody may not agree with it, but . . . the Word of God is upon me like fire shut up in my bones and when God gets upon me, I've got to say it. I've got to tell it all over everywhere. And God has called me to deliver those in captivity . . . I'm going to preach about it. I'm going to fight for them. I'll die for them if necessary . . .[34]

Preaching prophetically in the Christian tradition requires the deeper conversion of the preacher to the reality of the Gospel as it is hidden in the profound mystery of the cross of Jesus Christ. As King explained,

> Christianity has always insisted that the cross we bear precedes the crown we wear. To be a Christian one must take up his cross, with all of its difficulties and agonizing and tension-packed content and carry it until that very cross leaves its marks upon us and redeems us to that more excellent way which comes only through suffering.[35]

Preaching Paul prophetically honors the pastor-prophet Paul, because it honors Jesus Christ. Whenever we seek to follow the lead of the biblical text, and in this case, to follow in the steps of the biblical author, it is not for the sake of the text itself (the letters that Paul wrote, however valuable) or for the sake of Paul himself (however important), but because in their witness to Jesus Christ they point to the Subject of all the biblical texts and the Lord of all the biblical writers.

A. Katherine Grieb is associate professor of New Testament
at Virginia Theological Seminary, Alexandria, Virginia.

---

34. King, "Guidelines for a Constructive Church," sermon given June 5, 1966, at Ebenezer Baptist Church, Atlanta, cited in Cone, op. cit., 242. See also Richard Lischer's *The Preacher King: Martin Luther King, Jr. and the Word That Moved America* (Oxford: University Press, 1995).

35. King, January 17, 1963, National Conference on Religion and Race, Chicago, quoted in Garrow, *Bearing the Cross*, 532.

EPILOGUE: JESUS, THE PROPHET

John 3:1–17
Lent 2 A
Rhonda Smith McIntire

"THE LIFE of a prophet is no bed of roses." That phrase has been running through my mind of late.

Let's be clear about what a prophet is and is not. Prophets are not fortune-tellers. Predicting the future is not what prophets do. Rather, prophets of our Judeo-Christian tradition are primarily concerned with the present, with God's message for right now, with summoning people to respond to God *today*.

In Greek, the word *prophet* literally means *one who speaks for another*, especially for a deity. A prophet communicates the divine will. A prophet is an intermediary, a spokesperson, one sent by God to act and speak on behalf of God.

Like Miriam and Elijah and Deborah and Jeremiah and Isaiah and Isaiah's wife and so many others from the Hebrew Testament. Like John the Baptist and Anna from the New Testament. Like Gandhi and Desmond Tutu and Betty Friedan and Martin Luther King, Jr. and Rosa Parks and Cesar Chavez from the last century. Like Jesus and the prophets throughout all time, whose prophetic lives were aimed at saving the world and whose prophetic lives were no bed of roses.

With very few exceptions, prophets begin by telling us about God's vast love for us, then they urge us to respond to that love with social justice and ethical living. And, with very few exceptions, people love to hear about God's love, but they get tired of hearing about God's call for social justice and ethical living. And, then, people tend to take out anger and fear and frustration on the prophets. Those described in Scripture as "chosen" by God, often as not, live broken lives. No bed of roses.

Gary Meade, ordained to the sacred order of priests yesterday, vowed to follow Jesus, the prophet. Father Meade vowed "to proclaim by word and deed the Gospel of Jesus Christ," to be a prophet among you. And, I know you will love it when Gary tells you of God's love. But I wonder if you will get tired of the part of the message that also proclaims your duty to bring about justice for all people? I wonder if Gary's ministry among you will be a bed of roses?

A parishioner who has vowed to follow Jesus the prophet, said the other day, "Rhonda, I believe the smelly homeless people in our lobby are just as important as the people who can afford to eat at fancy restaurants." Will we offer him a bed of roses?

Another parishioner, who vows to follow Jesus the prophet, said about six months ago, "I'm afraid the Cathedral's endowment is more of a curse than a blessing. God's people are in need. I worry that we are sinful to hoard our millions." I haven't heard her say that lately. When she did, I doubt if she was offered a bed of roses.

Then, there's an African bishop who follows Jesus the prophet, who told a group of chic-chic Washingtonians in a tony Georgetown living room, "My people don't want you to give your money for us; we want you to give your lives for us." Did he sleep on a comfy bed of rose petals that night?

About ten years ago, I heard of a Roman Catholic priest in Amarillo, Texas, who follows Jesus the prophet. It was when all the big lawsuits against Pantex were being settled in favor of hundreds of people who were dying of cancer caused by drinking the water supply Pantex had polluted for decades of profit-making. Many of this priest's congregants worked for Pantex, and they followed Jesus the prophet, and they were heartsick at what their company had done. The priest stood in the pulpit one Sunday and proclaimed, "It is time to stand up against big industry that puts profit above people. If any of you choose to quit your jobs at Pantex, I promise you the church will provide you with shelter and food until you get settled again." There was no bed of roses for that priest—not in Amarillo or in his next parish in another state, to which he was reassigned about forty days later.

I read an article not long ago (I would give anything if I had saved it) that quoted a "feminist economist" (and, of course, I liked the "feminist" part!). The author noted that whenever she spoke publicly about women in the workplace, someone would inevitably comment: "At least things are better than they used to be." The economist professed her frustration with those who content themselves with the slow pace of change and wondered why *what has been* is so often used as the yardstick of progress, rather than *what might be*. I seriously doubt that her hotel room at conferences she addresses comes with the amenity of a bed of roses.

Jesus the prophet tells us God loves us immeasurably and we say, "Oh, thank you, Jesus. May we give you a bed of roses?"

Then Jesus the prophet tells us to turn the other cheek, to give the poor the clothes off our backs, to love our enemies, to forgive seventy times seven, to do the good we do in secret, to minister to criminals. Jesus says, "Do not judge." He says, "Give to everyone who begs from you." He says, "You cannot serve God and wealth."

And, in the last line of today's Gospel, Jesus the prophet says, "I'm not here to condemn you but to show you the way of salvation."

And, we say, "Yeah, right, have we got a bed for you, Jesus. Not rose petals for the prophet we'd rather not hear. You know, roses have thorns, too."

And, every year, our Savior wears a crown of those thorns, because you and I still don't listen to the prophets.

Rhonda Smith McIntire is vicar of St. John's Church,
Chula Vista, California.

ACKNOWLEDGEMENTS

THE PUBLICATION of this annual series of selected sermons has been made possible by the contributions of many people. The editors wish to thank the preachers of the Episcopal Church who have submitted their work for our consideration.

We also wish to acknowledge the fine work of Morehouse Publishing for making it possible for us to present these sermons and essays in such an attractive form. *Sermons That Work: Vols. I–XII* is now the longest running annual anthology of sermons ever published.

We also wish to thank the Board of Directors of The Episcopal Preaching Foundation, Inc. Were it not for their continued interest and support, the *Sermons That Work* series would not exist.

The Mission Statement of The Episcopal Preaching Foundation, Inc., reads as follows:

"The Episcopal Preaching Foundation exists to promote and support the ministry of preaching in the Episcopal Church in the United States. The Foundation is an independent agency of the Church that works cooperatively with others who share a common vision. Excellence in preaching is our emphasis. To accomplish this, the Foundation provides theological education to seminarians and ordained clergy. In addition we promote good preaching in our parishes by finding and publishing fine sermons annually through our volumes in the Sermons That Work *series."*

The Episcopal Preaching Foundation is a completely independent organization. It is not funded by the offices of our denomination. Its work is entirely supported by the gifts of those laity and clergy who believe that excellent preaching is vital for the health and mission of the Episcopal Church.

For more information about the Foundation or to make a tax-free contribution of financial support to the Foundation, you may contact us at the address given below.

The Episcopal Preaching Foundation, Inc.
c/o The A. Gary Shilling Company
500 Morris Ave.
Springfield, NJ 07081-1021
Phone: 973.467.0070